AI Power in the Classroom

working smarter, improving outcomes

Terry Carr and Walter Patterson

Copyright © Terry Carr Consultancy Ltd

All rights reserved. No part of this publication may be reproduced stored in a retrieval system, or transmitted in any form, or by any means, electronic, mechanical, photocopying, recording or otherwise without the prior written permission, of the authors or publisher, nor be otherwise circulated in any form of binding or cover other than that which it is published and without a similar condition including this condition being imposed on the subsequent author or publisher.

First edition 2024
ISBN: 9798326630179

Cover design Mr Ross Douglas, Wallace High School, Scotland

Table of contents

AI Power in the Classroom i

working smarter, improving outcomes i

Preface vii
    Introduction vii
    About the authors viii

1: Introducing AI power in the classroom 1
    A brief history of AI 1
    What are the key concepts and techniques in AI? 2
    The integration of AI in everyday IT tools 3
    The potential impact of AI on education 3
    How are teachers using AI now? 4
    How are students using AI now? 5
    Further reading 6

2: Large language models and Generative AI 7
    7
    What are large language models? 7
    What is Generative AI? 8
    How can I access and use Generative AI? 8
    Are there other ways to get started on my AI journey? 9
    How can AI support student learning? 9
    Risks and pitfalls 11
    Custom GPTs 13
    Conclusion 14
    References and further reading 14

3: The AI teacher assistant 15
Curriculum and lesson planning 15
Developing rubrics and assessments 16
Assessments and quizzes 16
Data analysis 16
Reporting 17
Research 17
Conclusion 18
Case studies and real-world examples 19

4: Differentiating and personalising learning with AI 20
Using AI to tailor teaching and learning 20
Adaptive learning platforms 21
Personalised learning recommendations 23
Conclusion 24
References 24

5: AI for students with special educational needs 25
How do you start introducing AI tools to students with special educational needs? 25
How can you use AI to identify and support students with SEN? 26
AI-powered tools for personalised learning and accommodations 27
What should you tell parents? 28
What should you tell students? 28
What are the dangers of using AI for students with SEN? 29
Mitigating AI risks 29
Conclusion 30
References and further reading 30

6: AI for pastoral care and personal tutoring 31

The role of AI in supporting student wellbeing and pastoral care 31

Potential benefits and risks of Generative AI in pastoral care and personal tutoring 33

Conclusion 35

7: AI across the curriculum 36

Applications of AI in English and literacy 36

Applications of AI in Mathematics and numeracy 37

Applications of AI in Languages 38

Applications of AI in Science 40

Application of AI in Social Studies and Humanities 41

Applications of AI in Expressive Arts and Music 42

Applications of AI in Design, Technology and Computing 44

Applications of AI in Health and Wellbeing 45

Developing AI literacy and computational thinking 47

Responsible use of AI principles 47

Preparing students for AI-driven industries and careers 48

Conclusion 49

ANNEX 1 Using ChatGPT 50

Generative AI and archiving 57

Custom instructions 58

Example of enabling custom instructions 59

Develop your prompting skills 60

Using Generative AI to improve prompts 61

Replicating your voice 61

ANNEX 2 Curriculum and lesson planning 64

Curriculum planning 64

Lesson planning 67

ANNEX 3 Developing rubrics 72

ANNEX 4 Assessments and quizzes 76

ANNEX 5 Data analysis 78

ANNEX 6 Reporting: enhancing teacher-parent communication 80

ANNEX 7 Research 84

ANNEX 8 Generative AI prompts by topic 87

English and literacy 87

Mathematics and numeracy 91

Languages 93

Science 95

Social Studies and Humanities 97

Expressive Arts and Music 100

Design, Technology and Computing 103

Health and Wellbeing 105

Glossary 109

Preface

'We don't need to fear the future of AI. We need to shape it.'

Audrey Tang, Minister for Digital Transformation, Taiwan (World Economic Forum)

Introduction

We have written this book to help you use artificial intelligence (AI) well in school. It is for teachers—all teachers—all who engage with a class every day. By this, we mean teachers of all stages of education—early years, primary/elementary, secondary/high school, special education, and higher education.

It is for those of you who have not yet dipped your toe into the swirling AI waters and also for those of you who have used many of the popular apps, such as ChatGPT, CoPilot and the expanding range of AI-enhanced software packages.

We strongly believe that you should start using AI technology now to improve the work you are doing in school. You shouldn't wait until some unknown future maturity date for AI technology. Starting now will help you to learn AI's strengths and its pitfalls.

This book will save you time on your everyday tasks. Experienced AI users may find some new ways of using AI that can help their students make even better progress. We have also written this to help you create new learning experiences in your classrooms that are conducive to learning and will help you evolve your teaching style in an AI-infused world.

We have included many examples and step-by-step instructions to help you develop your skills in using AI. Annex 1 to Annex 8 contain examples of templates that are relevant to different stages of education; they include a wide range of curriculum areas. We also tell you how you can use AI to help your students with special educational needs (SEN) and those who need personal support.

Throughout, we emphasise the safe and ethical use of AI for you and your students.

Many governments, education authorities, other school providers, school governors and school leaders are looking for ways to manage the introduction and safe use of AI in their schools. We hope this book will help them to accomplish this challenging task.

About the authors
Terry Carr and Walter Patterson are passionate about improving children's and young people's education outcomes by using technology. They taught in schools and colleges in Scotland and used digital technology innovatively to improve student outcomes. Both have Masters degrees and both worked as HM Inspectors of Schools in Scotland. Now, they work as international education consultants, advising government departments, school owners, headteachers and other leaders and teachers on how they can improve teaching and student outcomes.

Terry and Walter have prepared a companion blog – theaipoweredclassroom - to keep you updated on important developments in the use of AI in education.

Scan the QR code with your phone to access the blog or enter the URL into your browser.
https://theaipoweredclassroom.org

1: Introducing AI power in the classroom

'AI promises to be a powerful ally for teachers, providing them greater capacity to nurture the human connections with students that are foundational to learning.'

Linda Darling-Hammond, President and CEO of the Learning Policy Institute

perform tasks that would otherwise require human intelligence, for example, summarising a chapter of a book. While the concept of AI has been around since the 1950s, AI has seen major advances and more practical applications in recent years.

A brief history of AI

The foundations of AI date back to the 1950s when mathematicians and scientists began exploring the possibilities of machines processing logic and reasoning like the human brain. In the 1960s and 1970s, research labs at universities, including Massachusetts Institute of Technology (MIT), Stanford and Carnegie Mellon, worked on developing AI systems that could solve a wide range of problems. However, this early research did not lead to many useful applications due to limitations in processing power and data and overly ambitious goals.

In the 1980s, AI research shifted to more narrowly defined applications, like expert systems for specific domains. This type of software was created to solve specific problems, such as troubleshooting a car engine that does not start. The late 1990s and 2000s saw the rise of machine learning, in which AI systems and their algorithms are trained on large amounts of data rather than programmed with predefined rules. The availability of huge volumes of data (big data) and computing power advances enabled machine learning breakthroughs. In the 2010s, deep learning[1] using neural networks sparked new waves of progress in image and speech recognition, natural language processing (NLP), and other AI capabilities. Mustafa Suleyman provides a succinct history of AI development (Suleyman and Bhaskar, 2023)[2].

AI is a powerful technology that will have a significant impact on our lives and work. It has been compared to electricity, as it will extend and amplify our abilities. Just as the development of electricity from its early use as a source of light led to the creation of motors, generators, transistors, and microchips, AI will have a similar impact on our world and is advancing quickly.

What are the key concepts and techniques in AI?
Key concepts and techniques that enable modern AI systems include:

- machine learning algorithms that can learn and improve from data, without being explicitly programmed
- neural network computing systems that are modelled on the human brain's neural structure
- natural language processing that enables computers to understand, interpret and generate human language
- computer vision that enables computers to identify and process visual inputs like images and videos

---

[1] A glossary of technical terms is included at the end of the book.

[2] Suleyman, M and Bhaskar, M. (2023). *The Coming Wave*. Bodley Head.

- robotic machines that can carry out complex physical tasks
- expert AI systems that are designed to replicate and surpass human-level expertise in specialised domains, such as medicine, engineering, finance, and law

We explore the significance of these concepts and techniques to education in later chapters.

The integration of AI in everyday IT tools

Many familiar consumer technology products now rely on AI. Web search engines use AI to improve results. Writing support tools, such as Grammarly and Quillbot, provide real-time suggestions to improve writing. Smartphone apps like digital assistants, translators, and photo image software all make use of AI. Social media platforms employ AI for content recommendations and moderation. AI also enables facial recognition, autonomous driving technology, personalised advertising, and more.

The potential impact of AI on education

As AI becomes more widespread, it is poised to transform education. Some key applications for teachers include:

- intelligent tutoring systems that can adapt to students' individual learning needs and styles
- natural language technology that enables learning through conversations between students and chatbot software applications
- AI-automated grading of student submissions and assignments with real-time feedback

- personalised education provided by AI analysis of individual student strengths and areas for improvement
- AI powering virtual reality environments that create engaging immersive educational experiences

How are teachers using AI now?

The use of AI by teachers is rapidly increasing. The information available suggests that teachers are already using AI in their professional lives and in their classrooms. A 2023 report[3] outlining the use of ChatGPT in the USA confirms this trend and provides examples.

Creating content

Teachers are generating course materials, worksheets, and quizzes using AI. Increasingly, they are creating images and voice-overs for presentations.

Finding creative solutions

Teachers are using AI to find innovative approaches to teaching and learning that are more engaging and interactive. AI helps them to brainstorm ideas and receive feedback.

Analysing class data

Teachers are conducting rapid data analysis and receiving timely feedback on areas for improvement by uploading data such as student survey results and assessment outcomes.

---

[3] Walton Family Foundation (2023). *Teachers and students embrace ChatGPT for education*. Available at:
https://www.waltonfamilyfoundation.org/learning/teachers-and-students-embrace-chatgpt-for-education (Accessed: March 2024).

Communicating
Teachers are deploying AI to be more effective and efficient in constructing messages and communicating. They are using AI to generate messages in a given style, including their own writing style. AI systems can also translate and read aloud messages in a variety of languages, making communicating in a multilingual class more accessible and inclusive.

Automating repetitive tasks
Teachers are using AI tools to transcribe recorded sessions with students and summarise the key themes. They also dictate notes to an AI tool and use it to improve the readability of the text or adjust it for a certain age range.

This book focuses on practical applications of these ideas in a range of education settings, from early years to higher education. The worked examples and templates will help you to exploit AI today and in the future.

How are students using AI now?

Students are adept at using technology to make their lives easier and more fun, but there is a current lack of research on how students actually use AI at home under their own initiative. An article by Chan and Hu (2023)[4] suggests that the way older students use AI depends strongly on their attitude toward their own learning. In short, are they trying to deepen their learning, or are they trying to cut corners? This article

---

[4] Chan, C. and Hu, W. (2023). 'Students' voices on generative AI: perceptions, benefits, and challenges in higher education,' *International Journal of Educational Technology in Higher Education.* Available at: https://educationaltechnologyjournal.springeropen.com/articles/10.1186/s41239-023-00411-8 (Accessed March 2024).

highlights the need for us to help students use AI to enhance their learning safely and ethically.

The use of AI in education also raises important challenges around the privacy of data, preventing bias, and maintaining accountability. This needs to be addressed thoughtfully but, when harnessed responsibly, AI has the potential to enhance learning and teaching in ways that are ever-expanding in their scope and impact.

The practical guidance we provide for implementing AI tools will save time and improve teaching and learning. And critically, it will help you to avoid the common and not-so-common pitfalls that lie in the path of the unwary AI user.

Further reading
Office of Educational Technology (2023) *Artificial Intelligence and the Future of Teaching and Learning*. Available at: https://tech.ed.gov/ai-future-of-teaching-and-learning (Accessed: March 2024).

2: Large language models and Generative AI

'Artificial intelligence and generative AI may be the most important technology of any lifetime.'

This chapter discusses the relationship between large language models (LLMs) and generative AI (GenAI). It contains a link to help you start using AI now. We describe in broad terms how you can avoid the pitfalls and dangers of using AI and identify recent

What are large language models?

Large language models (LLMs) are AI systems trained on massive text datasets, enabling them to predict text sequences efficiently and with high accuracy. Their advanced natural language capabilities allow LLMs to mimic human-like writing and hold conversations, making them versatile educational tools. LLMs stand out from earlier AI systems because of their ability to understand context, generate coherent and relevant text, and engage in dynamic interactions.

A specific subset of LLMs is called generative pre-trained transformers (GPTs). GPT models are fine-tuned to apply to a wide range of problems beyond language processing. The most well-known GPT at the time of writing is OpenAI's ChatGPT. Other GPT examples include Google's Gemini, Microsoft's Copilot and Anthropic's Claude.

What is Generative AI?

Generative AI refers to any system that can generate new content, such as text, images, audio, and video. The annexes provide specific examples of several generative AI systems.

The relationship between generative AI and LLMs is illustrated below. This diagram is an amended version of one that appeared in a recent UK Government report.[5]

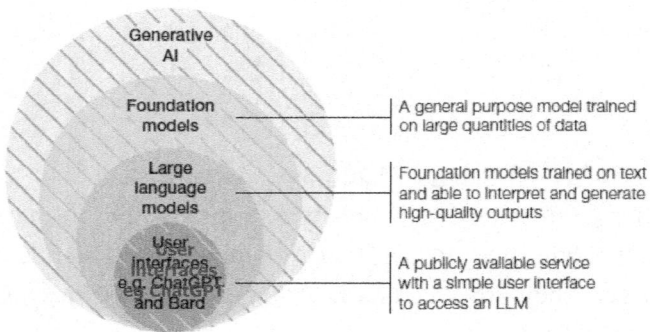

The relationship between Generative AI and GPTs

How can I access and use Generative AI?

The first step is to open an account with a company offering access to a generative AI product. At present, several products, such as ChatGPT from OpenAI or Claude from Anthropic, allow some free access.

You communicate with a generative AI product by typing a prompt into a chatbot interface and you receive a response in seconds. Crafting

---

[5] Central Digital and Data Office. (2024) *Generative AI Framework for HMG (HTML)*. Available at: https://www.gov.uk/government/publications/generative-ai-framework-for-hmg/generative-ai-framework-for-hmg-html (Accessed March 2024).

effective prompts involves setting context and constraints and specifying the desired output format and tone. You can find helpful prompts and templates online in forums and blogs.

Have a look at Annex 1 on page 50 to start using AI.

Further details, step-by-step examples, and advice on creating helpful prompts for education are available in the Annexes. You can also find updated examples of prompting in our blog 'AI Power in the Classroom'.[6]

Are there other ways to get started on my AI journey?

Recent months have also seen many AI enhanced apps emerge. Hundreds of apps are available that provide custom interfaces to underlying LLMs. These apps use your responses to questions to construct complex prompts. These prompts are then used to generate responses that meet your educational needs. These apps can help generate responses for different aspects of education, such as lesson planning, assessment, and curriculum content. One current example is Teachermatic[7]. This app is designed for teachers and provides easy access, through an attractive user interface. It can generate assignments, quizzes, presentations and routine tasks. However, it is important to note that apps are not immune from the problems of bias and unreliability that exist in the LLMs themselves.

How can AI support student learning?

Students can use AI to support their learning in the following ways:

---

[6] Carr, T. and Patterson, W. (2024) *AI Power in the Classroom*. Available at https://theaipoweredclassroom.org (Accessed March 2024).
[7] Teachermatic. Available at: https://teachermatic.com/ (Accessed March 2024).

- AI can provide an individualised approach for students that helps to reinforce concepts and bridge knowledge gaps. For instance, a student struggling with fractions might receive additional practice problems with step-by-step guidance, while another more proficient student might be challenged with more complex problems.

- AI can identify patterns in a student's writing, such as common grammatical mistakes or stylistic inconsistencies, and offer targeted advice to help them improve their writing skills.

- AI can make learning more interactive through conversational quizzes, where students receive immediate feedback. Recent advances support voice recognition and computer-generated speech.

- AI can simplify complex concepts, acting as an 'on-demand' expert. It can provide explanations tailored to students' current level of understanding.

- AI can help students with brainstorming and generating creative writing ideas and plot developments.

- The 24/7 availability of AI enables it to act as an on-demand source of help and assistance for students.

- AI can provide individual tuition to language students in their target language and assist them in understanding grammar through graded exercises and individualised feedback.

You can use AI to support students' learning:

- You can create interactive fiction scenarios linked to course concepts, to simulate conversations with historical figures or

literary characters and provide a unique perspective on historical events or narratives.
- Automated grading systems and objective feedback can save you time. You can train AI algorithms to identify specific errors or patterns in student work, allowing you to provide targeted feedback relevant to the assignment.

Risks and pitfalls

It is important to understand that there are potential pitfalls when integrating AI into your classroom. Recognising and mitigating these risks allows you to harness the benefits of AI safely and ethically.

There are risks that you should be aware of:

- Generative AI systems can produce false or misleading information. This is a major shortcoming that can trip up novice users of this technology. Many users find it too easy to accept the plausible, well-written statements that generative AI systems can produce. This effect is generally known as a 'hallucination'.
- To combat the spread of misinformation through LLM hallucinations, it is crucial for educators and students to approach AI-generated content with a critical eye:
    - **Verification**: always cross-check LLM-generated information against trusted sources, especially when accuracy is paramount.
    - **Awareness**: educate students about the nature of LLMs, emphasising that, while they are powerful tools, they are not infallible and can generate incorrect or false information.

- **Critical thinking**: encourage critical thinking skills that question and analyse the information provided by an LLM, fostering an environment where students learn to seek out multiple sources of information.

- The convenience and efficiency of AI can lead to over-reliance. The human elements of teaching, like empathy and understanding student needs, are irreplaceable. AI should complement, not replace, teachers.

- The use of systems that involve sharing student data raises privacy concerns. Laws and regulations on privacy, like the General Data Protection Regulation (GDPR) and the Family Educational Rights and Privacy Act (FERPA), must be followed strictly.

- Biases in training data can lead AI systems to generate unfair or prejudiced outcomes that are harmful to student evaluations or content. Teachers must mitigate bias proactively.

- While AI knowledge is amazingly extensive, it does have limits. LLMs are very expensive to create, and a particular LLM will only have knowledge up to the date it was created. Therefore, an LLM may generate outdated or inaccurate information. Continuous monitoring is vital to identify and correct any inaccuracies in information for use in education.

- Sophisticated language can falsely imply reliability and expertise. The authoritative tone of most AI systems can readily lull users into accepting generated information as being truthful. Students should know that AI does not truly 'understand' what it generates.

- Carefully crafted wording can trick AI into answering prompts that are not deemed ethical. You should read the output from generative AI in conjunction with its prompt sequence to detect such manipulation.

You can find a more detailed discussion of these ideas in a report on the future of AI in education (Hamilton et al., 2023).[8]

The providers of generative AI solutions are responding to concerns about data privacy by incorporating a feature that allows the user to instruct the LLM to 'forget' all information shared in a prompt session. This should help alleviate some concerns about data leakage when using AI.

Custom GPTs

A recent trend is the development of customised GPTs. LLMs are generally trained on a wide range of data that may not correlate to the specific needs of a knowledge domain. Custom GPTs allow fine-tuning of domain-specific data that incorporate domain terminology, such as in mathematics. They can also be fine-tuned to provide output in certain forms. ChatGPT has a custom GPT catalogue that includes Tutor Me (Khan Academy)[9], Mia AI[10], and Academic Assistant Pro[11]. These apps are more accessible for new users of AI who are interested in a particular area of learning.

Custom GPTs that are trained on well-curated, valid and limited data sets enable organisations like national curriculum services and examination

---

[8] Hamilton, A., Wiliam, D. and Hattie, J. (2023) *The Future of AI in Education: 13 things we can do to minimize the damage.* Available at: https://osf.io/preprints/edarxiv/372vr (Accessed March 2024).
[9] Tutor Me (Khan Academy). Available at: https://chat.openai.com/g/g-hRCqiqVlM-tutor-me (Accessed March 2024).
[10] Mia AI. Available at: https://heymia.ai/ (Accessed March 2024).
[11] Academic Assistant Pro. Available at: https://chat.openai.com/g/g-Ej5zYQRIB-academic-assistant-pro (Accessed March 2024).

boards to develop AI systems with reliable, validated outputs. South Australia has used this feature in a custom GPT (EdChat) to create a 'walled garden' GPT for use in its schools. This ensures that there is no leakage of school data back to a public GPT and permits only certain types of content to be available to its students.

Conclusion

While AI offers exciting opportunities to enhance learning, it must be implemented with a critical eye towards the potential risks and pitfalls. Educators play a crucial role in mediating the relationship between students and technology. They should ensure that the integration of AI into the classroom is beneficial and aligns with core values. Government departments, education authorities and school districts are now developing and publishing guiding principles for the safe use of AI in their schools. Teachers should always operate in accordance with that guidance. Teachers and students must work together to ensure that using AI in the classroom remains complementary to, rather than a replacement for, critical human judgement and authoritative knowledge.

References and further reading

Department for Education. (2023) *Generative artificial intelligence (AI) in education.* Available at: https://www.gov.uk/government/publications/generative-artificial-intelligence-in-education#full-publication-update-history (Accessed March 2024).

Ross, E.M., Harvard Graduate School of Education. (2023) *Embracing Artificial Intelligence in the Classroom,* Available at: https://www.gse.harvard.edu/ideas/usable-knowledge/23/07/embracing-artificial-intelligence-classroom (Accessed March 2024).

3: The AI teacher assistant

'It'll be unthinkable not to have intelligence integrated into every product and service. It'll just be an expected, obvious thing.'

in the classroom. Teacher assistant AI can automate administrative tasks, provide data-driven insights, and even assist with core teaching activities. This chapter explores how an AI teaching assistant could enhance curriculum planning, assessment, data analysis, and reporting.

Curriculum and lesson planning

An AI assistant could help generate lesson plans and curriculum that are sequenced to the needs and knowledge of a group of students or an individual student. AI could extract standards and learning objectives from school or national source documents, assess current student attainment levels, and suggest engaging content formats like discussion prompts, interactive fiction, and mixed media. This personalised lesson planning based on data would save teachers time while optimising the learning experience. However, lesson and curriculum plans created this way may have factual errors or be based on inappropriate pedagogical foundations. Nevertheless, using AI can provide very useful first drafts or starting points.

Look at some examples in Annex 2 on page 64.

Developing rubrics and assessments
AI can automate the creation of assignments, quizzes, and rubrics tailored to curriculum goals and student needs. The AI assistant could suggest varied assessment formats, such as essays, multiple-choice questions, presentations, or projects, to suit different learning styles and subjects. AI's objectivity and scalability could help address assessment bias and excessive teacher workload.

Look at some examples in Annex 3 on page 72.

Assessments and quizzes
AI can provide essay scoring and feedback generation and create dynamic multiple-choice questions based on student understanding. This use of AI can provide real-time monitoring of students' progress and understanding of the work at hand. AI tutors could also lead quiz sessions, adapting question types and difficulty in real time based on student responses and needs. Automated scoring and analysis could reduce teachers' workload while supporting frequent, transparent assessments.

Look at some examples in Annex 4 on page 76.

Data analysis
AI teaching assistants could compile and analyse student performance data to identify learning gaps. They could run comparisons against standards or trends, for example flagging a decrease in reading comprehension. Granular data could inform personalised improvement, interventions, and ability grouping. Teachers would retain decision authority while leveraging AI's superior data processing. The interactive nature of many AI tools enables teachers without advanced data analysis skills to make sense of large amounts of data, ask questions about trends

in students' performances over time, and compare their performances with external standards.

As indicated earlier, it is important to be cautious when sharing student performance data with an AI system. Student data is confidential, and sharing this data with third-party tools can pose risks to students' privacy and security. It is important to ensure that the ownership of the data is clearly defined and that the AI system complies with data protection regulations.

Look at some examples in Annex 5 on page 78.

Reporting

AI can streamline the reporting process by generating comprehensive reports and visual dashboards that illustrate student progress and outcomes. These AI tools can offer a clear view of student achievements and challenges, making it easier for you to communicate results to students, parents, and administrators. AI could populate reports with insights on student growth, trends, cohort analyses, and recommendations, saving you preparation time.

Look at some examples in Annex 6 on page 80.

Research

An AI assistant can be very helpful in carrying out research. We can expect generative AI to be more accurate in the future. However, at present, outputs need to be checked. Bing CoPilot, for example, claims that it currently produces validated outputs. All AI tools should be asked to reference their sources. AI can help to provide structures and first drafts of reports and papers. It can be used effectively to summarise and compare documents, pointing out common agreements and differences.

AI can very helpfully reformat information into tables, making it easier to understand complex information.

The experience of looking up information online, exploring content, and finding answers is changing. Tools like Perplexity AI are designed as answer engines. This is very different from the usual web search, which produces a list of web links for you to choose from and then continue your inquiry. As technology rapidly advances, you and your students are much more likely to explore information through a chatbot than a traditional web search.

Look at some examples in Annex 7 on page 84.

Conclusion
AI teacher assistants have immense potential to support you and improve outcomes through automated workflows, data-driven insights, personalised content and faster feedback. However, you must monitor AI output for bias, retain decision authority, and prioritise higher-order tasks. With human oversight, AI has the potential to unlock educational advances to benefit all students.

Case studies and real-world examples
Suggestions for further reading include:

- Jill Watson: a virtual teaching assistant developed by Georgia Tech that helps answer student inquiries in large classes.[12]
- Thinkster Math: combines AI with real tutor feedback to personalise student learning in Mathematics.[13]
- Carnegie Learning: offers AI-driven assessments and adaptive learning technologies that have been shown to support student growth in various subjects.[14]

---

[12] Georgia Tech. (2016) *Meet Jill Watson: Georgia Tech's first AI teaching assistant.* Available at: https://pe.gathech.edu/blog/meet-jill-watson-georgia-techs-first-ai-teaching-assistant (Accessed March 2024).

[13] Thinkster. *Thinkster Math.* Available at: https://hellothinkster.com (Accessed March 2024).

[14] Carnegie Learning, Inc. (2024) *Carnegie Learning.* Available at: https://www.carnegielearning.com (Accessed March 2024).

4: Differentiating and personalising learning with AI

'New AI tools are enabling teachers to understand the strengths and gaps in a student's knowledge with greater precision, allowing us to individualise instruction in ways not previously possible.'

Jal Mehta, Professor of Education, Harvard Graduate School of Education

One of the most promising applications of AI in education is its potential to enable personalised and differentiated learning that is tailored to each student's distinct needs, abilities, interests and learning styles. This chapter explores various approaches for leveraging AI to provide customised and self-directed learning pathways for every student.

Using AI to tailor teaching and learning

Teachers face a major challenge in trying to meet the diverse learning needs of their students. AI systems can help you to differentiate learning in powerful ways. You should write explicit prompts or use the features of an available AI tool or platform that is designed for this purpose. Here are some ways AI can help:

- AI-enhanced lesson planning tools can offer a variety of learning activities, project ideas, and discussion questions that cater to diverse learning needs in a classroom. These tools are designed to adapt to different age groups or achievement levels.
- Diagnostic assessments powered by machine learning algorithms can evaluate each student's work in real time, to

pinpoint individual strengths, gaps in knowledge and areas for growth. This enables you to target your support precisely, to align with each student's learning potential.

- Intelligent tutoring systems and educational apps powered by AI can modify teaching strategies and how feedback is provided, based on real-time interactions with each student. This approach can provide engaging and individualised learning experiences.
- NLP enables conversations to take place between students and AI tutors. This enhances the personalisation of learning through responsive, interactive questioning.
- Learning management systems integrated with AI can send you automated alerts in real time. This lets you know if individual students need additional support or more challenging activities.
- AI algorithms can assess student profiles and provide evidence-based recommendations for groupings, pairings and assignments. This assists you in organising your classes and fostering more effective peer learning opportunities.

Clearly, AI has the potential to differentiate learning by continually processing individual student data and helping you to provide individualised support and challenge.

Adaptive learning platforms

Adaptive learning platforms (ALPs) are dedicated software programs that use AI to tailor learning experiences to the individual needs of each student. ALPs are designed to provide personalised instruction, real-time feedback, and data-driven insights into student progress.

In the USA, ALPs are being used in various school districts, including New York City, Los Angeles, and Chicago. Examples are Matific and DreamBox Math[15]. These are adaptive mathematics platforms that are available in many languages and used by over 4 million students globally. In several studies, DreamBox Math has been shown to be effective in improving student achievement in mathematics. Knewton Alta, an adaptive learning platform used in the USA, claims to be effective in improving student achievement in various subjects, including mathematics, science, and English.

A growing number of international schools are using ALPs. For example, Century Tech has been used successfully by several international schools in Dubai as a means of providing individualised homework for students. Khan Academy, an online learning platform, offers a variety of learning courses and has developed its own AI tutor (Khanmigo) to provide intelligent support to students. Another example is Coursera[16], an online learning provider that has developed a virtual coach (Coursera Coach) that can answer students' questions and share personalised feedback in real time. This AI coach can communicate in different languages at different education levels, creating a more inclusive and engaging experience for globally diverse students.

---

[15] Dreambox Learning, Inc. (2023) *DreamBox*. Available at: https://www.dreambox.com/ (Accessed March 2024).
[16] Coursera Inc. (2024) Available at: https://www.coursera.org/ (Accessed March 2024).

Personalised learning recommendations

In addition to differentiating teaching, AI systems can use data and converse with students to provide personalised learning recommendations tailored to each individual's needs. It can provide:

- curated lists of online practice problems, interactive tutorials, and hands-on exercises tailored to build each student's knowledge and skills from their current level

- recommendations for specific multimedia content like videos, podcasts, and self-paced modules targeted to individual students' developing capabilities and learning preferences

- personalised reading and resource recommendations, to enrich students' knowledge around their unique passions and interests linked to their current work

- careful selection of pairs or groups of students for peer learning projects and study sessions, based on complementary knowledge, skill sets and learning styles

- suggestions for real-world projects, hands-on maker challenges, field trip ideas, and workplace visits that will resonate with an individual student's strengths and goals

- customised practice assessments and formative quizzes designed to address knowledge gaps, with gradually increasing difficulty based on the student's progress

AI systems can optimise motivation, enrichment, and growth by aligning additional learning opportunities with each student's passions, needs, and demonstrated capabilities.

Conclusion

AI can adapt like a personal tutor to help students progress from their current level and achieve their potential. It tailors teaching and learning, provides dedicated adaptive learning platforms, and makes personalised learning recommendations. However, AI is not a 'silver bullet' or a substitute for a varied, rich learning programme.

AI does not replace whole-class and peer learning. Student privacy, agency, and socio-emotional development must remain a priority. Schools must also customise AI tools to avoid potential bias. With thoughtful implementation, AI personalisation promises to humanise learning while making it more student-centred, efficient, and impactful. This can help schools and teachers unlock every student's potential.

References

A Mathematics resource that has been proven to improve schools' results: SEGMeasurement. (2017) *An Evaluation of Matific Use in Grades Two and Three: A study of Matific product effectiveness.* Available at: https://www.matific.com/home/resources/media/documents/SEG-matific-study.pdf (Accessed March 2024).

An evaluation of different components of Matific's program: Henrietta Szold Institute. (2016) *Research Evaluation of "Matific".* Available at: https://www.matific.com/home/resources/media/documents/HS-matific-study.pdf (Accessed March 2024).

Bernacki, M. L., Greene, M. J., and Lobczowski, N. G. (2021) 'A systematic review of research on personalized learning: Personalized by whom, to what, how, and for what purpose(s)?' *Educational Psychology Review,* 33(4), 1675–1715. Available at: https://doi.org/10.1007/s10648-021-09615-8 (Accessed March 2024).

5: AI for students with special educational needs

'AI has the potential to dramatically expand access to high-quality, personalised learning opportunities for all students, especially those in parts of the world where quality teachers are scarce.'

Andreas Schleicher, Director for Education and Skills at the Organisation for Economic Co-operation and Development (OECD)

This chapter explores how AI can assist you in enhancing outcomes for students with special educational needs (SEN). AI has the potential to identify students with SEN and help you to plan their curriculum lessons, assessment, and learning adaptations. Along with mainstream peers, AI can provide personalised accommodations and support.

How do you start introducing AI tools to students with special educational needs?

To begin the process of using AI to help you and your students with SEN, you should:

- audit the current curriculum, activities and teaching tools to identify areas that could be enhanced with generative AI
- research AI applications that provide for SEN, and vendors with evidence of improved student outcomes
- start experimenting in one area with one AI tool
- develop an implementation roadmap, aligned with school values and policies

- seek commitment from senior leaders and cross-departmental input, and ask for assistance from IT staff
- provide transparency to parents and students about intended AI uses

How can you use AI to identify and support students with SEN?

AI-driven analytics can help you to identify students with SEN early, so you can initiate timely interventions for them:

- Algorithms can analyse classroom writing samples, speech patterns, and digital interactions, to detect early signs of dyslexia, dysgraphia or autism spectrum disorders.
- AI tutoring systems track student responses and knowledge gaps in real-time, flagging potential learning disabilities.
- Once identified, AI learning platforms provide personalised instruction, practice and feedback tailored to each student's needs and challenges.
- AI teacher assistants suggest assistive technologies and inclusive strategies suited to each student's strengths and needs.
- You can use AI to match appropriate specialist resources.

When used ethically, such AI applications enable proactive, personalised, evidence-based SEN identification and support.

AI-powered tools for personalised learning and accommodations

For students already identified as having SEN, AI can provide customised learning and accommodations, such as:

- adjustable text-to-speech and dictation tools that benefit those with dyslexia, executive function challenges or visual impairments
- virtual tutors that adapt teaching strategies to suit diverse learning styles and needs, including auditory or verbal, visual, or hands-on learning
- personalised multimedia content and format selections that provide multisensory learning experiences
- text summarisation and extraction tools that help students to digest and summarise subject matter at their reading level
- simple syntax, vocabulary and visual adaptations for students with comprehension challenges
- reinforcement, modelling, prompts and goal-setting tools that build executive function
- translations for English language learners and text to sign language for deaf students
- analytics dashboards for you to monitor inclusive classroom engagement

When thoughtfully designed, AI has immense potential to personalise learning for neurodiverse students and create more accessible, engaging education.

What should you tell parents?
You should explain to parents specifically how AI will enable more personalised and adaptive support that is tuned to address their child's unique needs and learning preferences. It helps if you can provide real examples of customised interventions that their child could soon benefit from.

Share information about the AI tools that you will be using to tailor educational activities, lesson types, and assignments to the needs of their child. You should also include any interactive AI-powered tools their child may use.

Provide parents with assurances around rigorous safeguards that will be in place to preserve their child's privacy and proactively monitor data security with AI systems. You should explain clearly the restricted access controls and user authentication policies set up by the school.

Establish clear channels for parents to provide regular feedback to the school. Use this feedback to continue enhancing the technology and fine-tuning its responsible implementation.

What should you tell students?
Candidly clarify that AI is not intended to replace teachers or peer support. Stress that it is an additional tool to help you provide more engaging and enjoyable learning experiences tailored to how each student learns best.

Show students how AI tools can benefit them by providing activities, assignments, and learning materials uniquely personalised to their interests and needs.

You should tell students the school will highly value their input and feedback for improving AI tools. Explain that their voices are important in using AI to improve their education.

What are the dangers of using AI for students with SEN?

If you use AI for students with SEN, you should be wary of some potential dangers:

- If you rely on AI too much, it could degrade essential human relationships and emotional nurturing and inhibit creativity.
- Dataset biases or flawed algorithms could propagate inequities — identifying and protecting vulnerable student groups is vital.
- With large volumes of personalised data, compromised security could significantly harm students through leaks or misuse.
- Accessibility issues pose barriers for students with motor, vision, hearing, and other disabilities. These need to be addressed to provide an inclusive environment.

Mitigating AI risks

You should audit the use of AI to prevent over-dependence on automation. Ensure that there is a balanced approach to using AI. Qualified teachers and counsellors are important for developing socio-emotional learning and human relationship-building.

Continually monitor model outputs of AI systems for biases against protected classes, with rigorous and expansive testing protocols. You should welcome external audits to build trust.

With guidance from IT specialists, you can implement state-of-the-art defences to safeguard access controls and monitor activities and transactions. Student data needs to be protected and encrypted.

Conclusion

With thoughtful safeguards against bias, plus human oversight, AI can make SEN identification and support more evidence-based, responsive and personalised. If implemented responsibly, AI has promising applications to enhance inclusion, accessibility and outcomes for all students with special education needs.

References and further reading

Few recent publications have evaluated AI's success in improving outcomes for students with SEN.

Mehta, P., et al. (2023) *Inclusion of Children With Special Needs in the Educational System, Artificial Intelligence (AI)*. Available at: https://www.igi-global.com/chapter/inclusion-of-children-with-special-needs-in-the-educational-system-artificial-intelligence-ai/331738 (Accessed March 2024).

6: AI for pastoral care and personal tutoring

'The key is to keep technology human-centered.'

Sundar Pichai, CEO of Google

This chapter summarises the emerging AI applications that show potential in their capacity to support student wellbeing, pastoral care and personalised tutoring. AI-powered chatbots, virtual counsellors and tutoring systems are being designed to provide individualised socio-emotional support and life skills coaching. However, caution is required when experimenting with this technology.

The role of AI in supporting student wellbeing and pastoral care

As a teacher, you understand that effective learning and academic success rely on strong socio-emotional skills, mental health and overall wellbeing. Claims that generative AI could assist students with pastoral care need to be evaluated carefully. The following claims have been made for the use of AI in pastoral care:

- Counselling chatbots can use NLP to allow students to confidentially discuss issues like bullying, anxiety or depression and receive personalised support 24/7. Typically, these chatbots check in regularly to ask how the student is doing, help them identify their emotions in difficult situations, and suggest relaxation exercises to work through the anxiety. These chatbots can respond immediately to issues that they identify.

- AI analysis of patterns in student writing samples, class participation and schoolwork can provide early warning signs of emerging problems like social isolation, low self-esteem or struggles with concentration. This will allow early intervention and support to be provided.
- Personalised socio-emotional learning activities can be tailored to each student's demonstrated strengths and growth areas, based on an analysis of tutoring interactions.
- Chatbot lessons can focus on building resilience, self-regulation, empathy, communication skills and other interpersonal capabilities.
- Meditation, mindfulness and cognitive behavioural therapy apps can use AI to adapt guidance to individual students' needs and progress.
- Virtual tutors can interactively model social skills and provide real-time feedback during group work, role-playing and other simulations.
- Immersive game-based environments can be used to safely practise conflict resolution, peer collaboration and teamwork competencies.
- Automated check-ins: teachers and staff can use AI tools to check in with students proactively. Sending personalised messages through email or institutional platforms helps maintain informal pastoral connections.

When thoughtfully implemented, such AI tools may provide students with personalised and equitable pastoral care. Typical tools that have been developed to support physical and medical health for adults include Cass[17], Wysa[18], and Woebot Health[19].

Potential benefits and risks of Generative AI in pastoral care and personal tutoring

The potential benefits of applying AI for student wellbeing and counselling include:

- increased access to affordable one-to-one support that schools often cannot otherwise provide
- the ability to personalise socio-emotional skill building and counselling to each individual student's needs and interests
- providing early, confidential assistance 24/7 through counselling chatbots
- surfacing data-driven insights to inform human counselling, advising and interventions

However, there are also risks that require careful management to mitigate any negative outcomes from the use of AI.

---

[17] Cass. Available at: https://www.cass.ai/ (Accessed March 2024).
[18] Wysa. Available at: https://www.wysa.com/ (Accessed March 2024).
[19] Woebot Health. Available at: https://woebothealth.com/ (Accessed March 2024).

These negative outcomes include:

- chatbots providing advice that may not be in line with the values of the school or the student's family.
- students becoming over-reliant on technology, instead of essential human relationships and interactions
- chatbots lack human judgement, empathy and nuance
- privacy concerns around sensitive student physical health, mental health and performance data
- the potential for emotional manipulation or biased recommendations from imperfect algorithms
- problematic content risks, with uncontrolled chatbot conversations

Responsible practices for schools implementing AI-driven pastoral care include:

- ensuring that student data is 'forgotten' by the AI and not stored or shared on public AI systems. This facility to not retain data is a feature of some generative AI systems
- ongoing student education on using AI tools appropriately and detecting potential harms
- human oversight and validation of any automated student evaluations or recommendations
- transparent use of student data, with clear consent and appeal processes
- customising tools to avoid racial, gender, cultural or other biases

- proactive auditing for risks like cyberbullying, self-harm content or predatory behaviour

When integrated thoughtfully and with necessary safeguards, AI could enhance inclusion, equity and support. But human connection and oversight should remain central to student wellbeing and learning.

Conclusion
It is essential to mitigate the risks of using AI for personal support and counselling. Human empathy and connection remain crucial, and schools should balance the use of technology and personal interactions to ensure holistic student support.

7: AI across the curriculum

'AI promises new methods for assessing student learning in the context of real-world problem solving, moving us toward evaluation and support better aligned with the demands of the 21st century.'

Linda Darling-Hammond, President and CEO of the Learning Policy Institute

curriculum areas. This chapter explores impactful applications of AI across core subject areas, while considering ethical implications and how to develop students' AI literacy. You can find practical xamples of detailed prompts in Annex 8 on page 87.

Applications of AI in English and literacy

Students of English language and English literature find certain aspects challenging, such as developing reading comprehension skills and avoiding grammatical errors in writing. Students come from different cultural backgrounds and can find it difficult to relate literary themes to their own contexts. A challenge that teachers of English and literacy often face is the time required to read student essays and provide feedback on aspects such as coherence and grammar. All of these are amenable to support from AI.

AI is transforming English language education in powerful ways:

- Adaptive reading apps tailor text difficulty to students' reading levels and provide definitions, pronunciations, and translations.

- Text summarisation and extraction tools help students to identify key ideas, supporting details and structural components.

- Intelligent writing assistants provide grammar correction, vocabulary suggestions and organisation feedback for student drafts.

- Chatbots engage students in interactive comprehension quizzes and literary analysis discussions.

- Chatbots can generate personalised reading and writing activities calibrated to each student's interests and academic level, to promote engagement and accelerated learning.

- Automated essay scoring can relieve teacher workloads, while providing instant formative feedback on aspects such as structure, grammar and style.

- Text-to-speech and dictation tools assist struggling readers and writers.

- Plagiarism detectors and citation recommendations promote academic integrity.

- Creative writing prompts and idea generators boost student engagement.

Used ethically, such AI literacy tools increase differentiation, engagement and agency, while building core skills.

Applications of AI in Mathematics and numeracy

In mathematics education, it is well understood that effective learning relies on securing an understanding of foundational knowledge, carefully sequencing the teaching of concepts and methods and providing regular opportunities for students to practice and apply their knowledge. AI has the potential to provide support for all these key elements by enabling:

- personalised assignment generators with problems targeted at students' skill levels
- immersive simulations and games for conceptual reinforcement
- virtual manipulatives that allow hands-on exploration of abstract concepts such as algebraic manipulation
- intelligent tutoring systems that adapt explanations and feedback to students' needs
- real-time assessment, with targeted remediation to fill knowledge gaps
- multimedia study guides combining videos, practice problems and quizzes
- activities to promote metacognitive reflection and mathematics discourse (for example think-pair-share)
- analytics to uncover student difficulties and inform differentiated instruction
- augmented reality to visualise complex geometry and calculus

Such AI mathematics tools promote active learning, comprehension and growth mindsets.

Applications of AI in Languages

The teaching of languages affords significant opportunities for AI to enrich the learning experience and give you a wide range of resources and approaches. AI is particularly suited to supporting vocabulary building and providing a 'just right' level of challenge that recognises the proficiency of individual students.

It is recognised that most students face challenges in preparing for speaking exams in language learning courses. The use of AI tools can offer innovative solutions to enhance your students' speaking skills, while ensuring compliance with age-appropriate guidelines.

AI also offers the opportunity to go beyond grammar rules and vocabulary and motivate students through engagement with popular culture in their chosen language. Here are some AI tools you can use:

- ChatGPT supports voice conversations in a wide range of languages, to provide conversational practice.

- Gliglish offers language learning by speaking with an AI tutor. It supports practising real-life situations to improve speaking and listening skills in various languages.

- Tutor Lily is an AI language tutor app that facilitates learning new languages through engaging conversations with a friendly AI companion. It provides a personalised learning experience, offering features like instant corrections, translations, and voice recognition for pronunciation practice. You can design comprehensive lesson plans by suggesting activities, resources, and methodologies tailored to different learning objectives and student proficiency levels.

With these tools, you can:

- generate worksheets, quizzes, and interactive exercises that can be customised for various language aspects, such as grammar, vocabulary, and cultural context

- propose diverse and engaging learning activities, from role-playing scenarios to language games, which can help in developing both speaking and reading skills

- simulate conversations, provide pronunciation practice, and give instant feedback, helping students to improve their spoken language abilities
- create reading materials at appropriate difficulty levels, offer comprehension questions, and even summarise texts to aid understanding

Note, however, that overreliance on AI risks reducing opportunities to develop intercultural communication skills. You must guide appropriate use.

Applications of AI in Science

You can use AI in your work as a science teacher to enhance your teaching materials and explanations, making complex scientific concepts more accessible and engaging for your students. Additionally, AI can save you valuable time by automating tasks such as generating practice problems, grading assignments, and providing additional support for research and learning.

For science education, AI enables:

- virtual labs with simulated experiments and open-ended discovery
- augmented and virtual reality, to foster immersive scientific exploration
- realistic virtual biological models, for safer dissections and investigations
- automated assessment of open-response questions and research reports

- intelligent study guides, with interactive diagrams, practice and feedback
- apps that use image recognition to identify plants, animals and rocks
- lifelike chatbots that simulate historical scientists and discoveries

Application of AI in Social Studies and Humanities

A key element in the teaching of social studies and humanities is helping students to think critically and see the interconnections between causes and effects. Grasping abstract concepts, such as justice, democracy, and culture, can be difficult for some students. One way that AI can help is by building student comprehension through conversational dialogue.

Relevant AI applications in social studies and humanities include:

- summaries of current news articles, to provide insights into global affairs and social issues, allowing students to stay informed and engaged with real-world events
- interactive lessons and quizzes for social studies topics, making learning engaging and motivating for students
- biographical information and historical context about significant figures in social studies, helping students to gain a deeper understanding of key individuals and their contributions
- discussion prompts and arguments for classroom debates and discussions on social and political topics, encouraging critical thinking and analysis

- immersive virtual reality trips visiting historical sites, museums, landmarks and re-enactments, allowing students to explore and learn about different cultures and periods
- simulating political systems, United Nations negotiations, and historical dilemmas that foster perspective-taking
- interactive maps with layered economic, social and political data representations
- intelligent quizzing on current and historical events that is tied to each student's progress
- chatbots that bring historical figures to life by simulating dialogue and questioning
- automated essay scoring with feedback on developing arguments and use of sources and evidence
- explanations and analyses of historical events, political movements, and social changes, helping students to understand the broader context and significance of historical occurrences
- geographical data to assist students understanding of the physical and human geography of different areas

Thoughtfully designed AI social studies tools spur critical thinking and historical empathy.

Applications of AI in Expressive Arts and Music

Developing technical skills in a creative context requires patience and perseverance to gain proficiency. Students can find this challenging and frustrating. They also frequently encounter creative blocks that require teacher intervention to resolve. AI can help to overcome challenges like these. By offering a dispassionate critique, it can help alleviate performance anxiety for students.

Emerging AI applications in expressive arts and music include:

- chatbots that provide art appreciation prompts to develop critical analysis skills
- AI-driven feedback systems that can offer instant, objective critiques of students' work, highlighting areas of strength and those needing improvement
- intelligent graphic design tools that provide students with formative feedback
- augmented reality apps that overlay artworks with contextual information
- algorithms that analyse musical compositions and suggest improvements
- music composition apps that allow students to input lyrics, genres, moods or basic melodies and harmonies to auto-generate an entire original song arrangement
- co-creative music apps that improvise with students in real-time
- tools that evaluate technique, timing, precision, and musicality as students practice instrumental pieces and prescribe targeted exercises to overcome weak areas
- tools for experimenting with visual media compositions and generative art
- automated assessments that recognise originality in interpreting works
- apps that identify features like brush strokes to teach painting techniques

- AI tools that can assist in creating music by generating melodies, harmonies, and rhythms
- AI art generators that can inspire students by producing images based on descriptions, which students can then interpret or expand upon in their own artistic mediums
- AI that can simulate performances of student compositions, providing a platform for students to hear or see their work in a virtual context before actual production
- AI tools that can help students to understand the emotional or thematic content of a piece of music or art by analysing and providing insights into its components

AI provides engaging new mechanisms for fostering student creativity. By integrating AI into the curriculum, you can enhance the learning experience in expressive arts and music, providing students with the tools to explore their creativity in unprecedented ways.

You should discuss with students the ethical implications of using AI in creative processes, including questions of originality, copyright, and the role of the artist.

Applications of AI in Design, Technology and Computing

The study of computing requires students to grasp coding syntax and logic and apply computing concepts to real problems. Debugging code and fixing errors requires diligence and focus, and when students struggle with these, they can become disengaged.

AI has direct applications in building students' computational thinking and computer science skills, such as:

- coding assistants that provide real-time syntax help and debugging for students
- simulated hardware environments, where students can experiment with algorithms
- cybersecurity games and challenges, with adaptive learning built-in
- tools to teach core concepts like computer architecture, systems software and networking
- chatbots with which students build computer code through conversation
- automated assessment of coding projects, with personalised feedback
- game-based computational thinking challenges, such as programming puzzles and logic challenges that make abstract concepts more tangible
- augmented and virtual reality platforms for developing immersive apps
- collaborative project spaces to produce AI innovations that address social needs

AI empowers students to engage directly in applied computing and build their confidence and self-efficacy.

Applications of AI in Health and Wellbeing

Personal, social and health education (PSHE) requires teachers to have confidence in nuanced behavioural methods that can inspire lifestyle changes and the adoption of healthy habits in young people. This is made more difficult by the plethora of misguided advice that students will encounter online. AI tools can help address misinformation and provide individualised support to students from different cultural contexts.

For PSHE, AI enables:

- chatbots that empathetically answer student questions on sensitive topics while guaranteeing confidentiality
- apps to immediately fact-check online health claims and rate content credibility
- virtual health coaches that enable personalised conversations, to coach young people through goal setting and adoption of healthier lifestyle habits
- apps with personalised exercises, nutrition plans and mental health coping strategies
- simulations to practise social interactions, decision-making and conflict resolution
- early warning systems to detect mental health crises and bullying
- on-body sensors to track fitness activity, hydration and healthy habits
- augmented reality (AR) games that promote physical coordination and motor skills

AI wellbeing tools can provide timely data and support, while protecting privacy.

Developing AI literacy and computational thinking

As AI becomes pervasive, developing students' literacy, ethics and critical thinking around technology is essential. By implication, you should have sufficient confidence and competence in the safe and ethical use of AI to provide leadership to your students in developing their AI literacy. We want students to acquire skills in:

- understanding AI concepts like machine learning, neural networks and NLP
- recognising biases in data, algorithms and digital media
- evaluating the validity and limits of information filtered by AI
- understanding the societal impacts of AI on issues like ethics, law and jobs
- carrying out student-led projects that apply AI to benefit communities
- actively controlling and making decisions about how they use technology, rather than passive consumption

AI offers powerful mechanisms to engage students, but critical thinking skills must remain central to enable them to evaluate AI sources and outputs, while understanding that AI is a tool that requires human oversight.

Responsible use of AI principles

Throughout this book, we have emphasised the importance of ethical standards and intelligent human oversight when using AI in education.

Others have also emphasised this view. The following AI principles have been advocated and are discussed in detail by Microsoft[20]:

- Fairness: AI systems should treat all people fairly.
- Reliability and safety: AI systems should perform reliably and safely.
- Privacy and security: AI systems should be secure and respect privacy.
- Inclusiveness: AI systems should empower everyone and engage people.
- Transparency: AI systems should be understandable.
- Accountability: people should be accountable for AI systems.

The Australian Government has also published similar principles.[21]

Preparing students for AI-driven industries and careers
Education can help students navigate our AI-driven economic future by:

- providing career guidance on emerging roles in AI research, application design, ethics and policy
- teaching data literacy and analytics skills that are applicable across industries

---

[20] Microsoft AI. *Empowering responsible AI practices.* Available at: www.microsoft.com/en-us/ai/responsible-ai (Accessed March 2024).
[21] Australian Government Department of Education. (2023) *Australian Framework for Generative Artificial Intelligence (AI) in Schools.* Available at: https://www.education.gov.au/schooling/resources/australian-framework-generative-artificial-intelligence-ai-schools (Accessed March 2024).

- developing resilient mindsets that embrace innovation and lifelong learning
- fostering the creativity, collaboration, communication and problem-solving that is valued in human-AI partnerships
- creating economic and work-based learning opportunities in AI
- ensuring technical training is paired with ethics and human social skills

With careful foresight and preparation, schools can empower students to find purpose in and contribute to an AI-transformed workplace.

Conclusion

AI has immense potential to enhance teaching and learning across the curriculum. However, students still require human guidance, an ethical framework and collaboration skills — these are vital to navigating an AI future.

ANNEX 1 Using ChatGPT

1. If this is your first use of ChatGPT you should access the main OpenAI webpage (www.openai.com) and create a user account. The basic (free) account will suffice to make a start on using a generative AI system. If you've already done this, proceed to step 2.

2. Sign in to your OpenAI user account.

3. This (or similar) dialogue box appears:

> How can I help you today?
>
> Design a database schema
> for an online merch store
>
> Give me ideas
> about how to plan my New Years resolutions
>
> Make a content strategy
> for a newsletter featuring free local weekend events
>
> Recommend activities
> for a team-building day with remote employees
>
> Message ChatGPT...
>
> ChatGPT can make mistakes. Consider checking important information.

4. Give a command, for example, 'Describe the moon'. The output is provided almost immediately and indicated by a downward-pointing arrow. You can copy the answer using the clipboard symbol beneath the text.

ChatGPT:

The Moon is Earth's only natural satellite and is one of the most prominent objects in the night sky. It has fascinated humans for centuries, and here are some key characteristics and information about the Moon:

1. Appearance: The Moon appears as a bright, silvery-white, or greyish disk in the night sky when it reflects the Sun's light. Its surface is marked by a variety of features, including dark areas called maria, which are large, flat plains, and bright areas known as highlands, which consist of rugged terrain. The Moon also has numerous impact craters, mountains, and valleys.

2. Size and Distance: The Moon is relatively small compared to Earth, with a diameter of about 3,474 kilometres (2,159 miles), making it roughly 1/6th the size of our planet. It orbits Earth at an average distance of approximately 384,400 kilometres (238,855 miles).

3. Phases: The Moon goes through a cycle of phases as it orbits Earth. These phases include the new moon, first quarter, full moon, and last quarter, among others. These phases are the result of the changing angles between the Moon, Earth, and the Sun.

4. Gravity: The Moon has less gravitational pull than Earth, with its surface gravity being about 1/6th that of Earth's. This lower gravity makes objects on the Moon weigh much less than they do on Earth, which has important implications for lunar exploration.

5. Lack of Atmosphere: Unlike Earth, the Moon has a very thin and virtually non-existent atmosphere, often called an exosphere. This means there is no air to breathe, and the lunar surface is exposed to the harsh conditions of space, including extreme temperature variations and cosmic radiation.

6. Lunar Day and Night: A day-night cycle on the Moon, known as a lunar day, lasts about 29.5 Earth days. This extended day and night are due to the Moon's slow rotation on its axis, which takes about the same amount of time as its orbit around Earth.

7. Exploration: The Moon has been the target of both robotic and crewed space missions. The Apollo program, run by NASA, successfully landed astronauts on the Moon between 1969 and 1972, with a total of six manned missions. Recent lunar exploration efforts have focused on robotic missions and plans for future human missions and lunar bases.

> 8. Impact History: The Moon's surface is heavily cratered, indicating a history of collisions with meteoroids and asteroids. Some of these impacts have created large basins, such as the South Pole-Aitken Basin, which is one of the Moon's largest impact features.
>
> In summary, the Moon is Earth's natural satellite, with a distinctive appearance, various surface features, and a role in human history and scientific exploration. It continues to be a subject of study and interest in both astronomy and space exploration.

This answer is general and may be inappropriate. This is because the prompt was not specific enough. This is known as zero-shot prompting, as we have asked a question without providing context.

We can now start a dialogue to get the information that we need. For example, we can ask, 'What does the moon look like?' and on a new line, obtained by pressing Shift-Return, enter 'Answer in no more than 50 words.'

(If you press Return by mistake rather than Shift-Return, ChatGPT will try to generate an answer to an unfinished question. You can stop the erroneous result by clicking on the small square inside a circle icon in the dialogue box.)

ChatGPT:

> The Moon appears as a greyish-white, silvery disk in the night sky, with visible surface features such as craters, mountains, and plains. Its appearance changes in a cycle of phases, from a thin crescent to a full, round disk, due to its changing position relative to the Earth and the Sun.

ChatGPT produced this 51-word paragraph and did not fulfil the request in detail. The dialogue can continue. We can ask again, for example, 'This answer is longer than 50 words. Please answer the question again.'

This time, a 37-word output is provided:

> The Moon appears as a silver-white, greyish disk in the night sky. Its surface features include craters, mountains, and plains. Phases range from a thin crescent to a full circle as it orbits Earth, reflecting sunlight differently.

When chatting with bots like ChatGPT, many people use pleasantries like 'please' and 'thank you' to make the dialogue more human-like. You can give ChatGPT feedback by using the thumbs-up and thumbs-down icons. You can repeat the same question using the regenerate symbol, and ChatGPT will ask if the second response is better, worse or the same as the first.

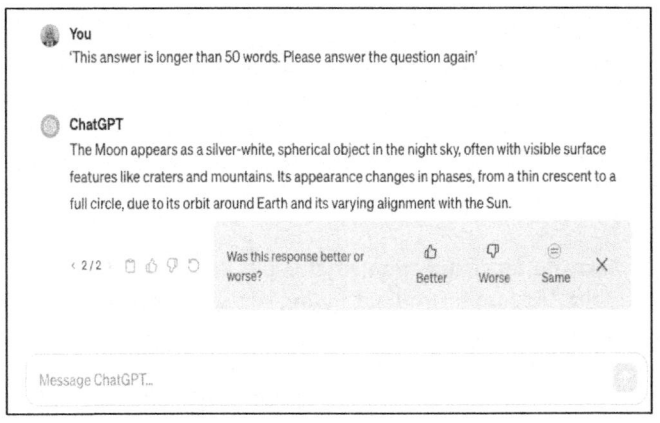

> **You**
> 'This answer is longer than 50 words. Please answer the question again'
>
> **ChatGPT**
> The Moon appears as a silver-white, spherical object in the night sky, often with visible surface features like craters and mountains. Its appearance changes in phases, from a thin crescent to a full circle, due to its orbit around Earth and its varying alignment with the Sun.
>
> ‹ 2/2 ›   Was this response better or worse?   Better   Worse   Same   ✕
>
> Message ChatGPT...

This example illustrates that each answer results from a statistical process, and it is important to set clear guidelines for the chatbot to get to the required result quickly.

Here is a prompt using the moon as the context for a school homework question.

You:

You are a teacher of 9-year-old students and want to check their understanding of the poem The Moon by Robert Louise Stevenson
<Start of poem>
The moon has a face like the clock in the hall;
She shines on thieves on the garden wall,
On streets and fields and harbour quays,
And birdies asleep in the forks of the trees.

The squalling cat and the squeaking mouse,
The howling dog by the door of the house,
The bat that lies in bed at noon,
All love to be out by the light of the moon.

But all of the things that belong to the day
Cuddle to sleep to be out of her way;
And flowers and children close their eyes
Till up in the morning the sun shall arise.

<End of poem>

Provide three questions that evaluate:
1. The students' understanding of the poem's vocabulary.
2. The use of simile.
3. The mood of the poem.
Ask the questions using a reading age of about 9 years.
For each question, provide an answer that the students would understand and make clear the links between the answer and the words or phrases used in the poem.

ChatGPT:

> Based on the poem "The Moon" by Robert Louis Stevenson, here are three tailored questions to check the understanding of 9-year-old students, along with answers that draw connections to the text:
>
> 1. **Understanding of the Poem's Vocabulary:**
>   **Question:** What does the word "thieves" mean in the line "She shines on thieves on the garden wall"?
>   **Model Answer:** "Thieves" are people who take things that do not belong to them. In the poem, this word means that the moonlight is shining on the garden wall where people who might be sneaking around can be seen.
>
> 2. **Use of Simile:**
>   **Question:** The poem begins with "The moon has a face like the clock in the hall." What does the moon's face and the clock's face have in common?
>   **Model Answer:** A simile is when you say something is like something else. Here, the poem says the moon's face is like a clock's face because both are round, and they both shine or glow, so you can see them in the dark.
>
> 3. **Mood of the Poem:**
>   **Question:** How do you think the poem wants us to feel about night time? Are there any words that make you think it's supposed to be a happy and peaceful time, or a scary time?
>   **Model Answer:** The poem makes night time seem like a happy and peaceful time. Words like "shines," "asleep," and "cuddle" make us feel that night is a time for rest and the moon is watching over everything kindly, not scary at all.
>
> These questions aim to evaluate specific aspects of the student's understanding in a manner that is approachable for their age group, guiding them to connect their answers with phrases directly from the poem.

This is a fair answer. Here is a regenerated version.

ChatGPT:

> Here are three questions tailored for 9-year-old students, based on Robert Louis Stevenson's poem "The Moon," along with answers that explain how they link to specific words and phrases in the poem:
>
> 1. **Understanding of the Poem's Vocabulary:**
>   **Question:** What does "squalling" mean when talking about the cat, and can you think of a time when you heard a cat make this sound?
>   **Model Answer:** "Squalling" means making a loud, harsh cry. It's the sound a cat makes when it's upset or angry. If you've ever heard a cat yowl when it's bothered or frightened, that's what squalling sounds like.
>
> 2. **Use of Simile:**
>   **Question:** The poem says "The moon has a face like the clock in the hall." What does this simile mean? How is the moon's face like a clock?
>   **Model Answer:** A simile is when we say something is like something else. The moon is like a clock because it has a round shape, and we can imagine it has numbers and hands moving around it, just like a clock.
>
> 3. **Mood of the Poem:**
>   **Question:** How does this poem make you feel? Is it supposed to be scary, happy, or calm and why? Look at the words used to describe the night and the moon to help you answer.
>   **Model Answer:** The poem feels calm and a little magical. Words like "shines," "asleep," and "cuddle" are soft and gentle. They make us picture a peaceful night where everyone is quietly resting, and the moon is watching over them.
>
> Each of these questions encourages the students to directly engage with the text, think critically about the language, and understand the emotional landscape of the poem.

This is a very similar answer. However, the format of the answer is not convenient to give to the students. You can ask ChatGPT to place the questions on one page and the answers on another. This illustrates that ChatGPT remembers the previous result, and you can ask for it to be refined or reformatted. It also shows that extended text can be entered into the dialogue box. This can be done directly or by copying and pasting a document in Word or PDF format into the dialogue box.

The emerging wisdom on good practice in prompting is that there is no single word or phrase that works consistently well. The essential features of writing good prompts are:

- Be clear and specific: state as clearly as you can what you want the AI to do.
- Provide the context: tell the AI the relevant background, including the purpose and audience of the output. For example, the answer should be understood by a 15-year-old student.
- Break down complex tasks into a series of simple steps. For example, ask the AI to do this, then this and this.
- State the format of the output: the tone, the language level and the structure. For example, use the same style as <provide a sample of text>
- Iterate and refine: ask the AI to clarify, elaborate or evidence its output.

Further and more complex examples are provided in the other Annexes.

Generative AI and archiving

Generative AI systems allow you to archive a chat session. In fact, this is the default mode for current generative AI systems. This means that you can return to an archived chat session, and the AI system will recall all the elements of your previous chat.

It is important to note that all the information you supply to a generative AI system is also archived and may be used by the system to improve its own performance and learning. This calls for caution in submitting student-generated work to this type of AI. Many AI systems now incorporate the facility to 'forget' and not save data.

Custom instructions

ChatGPT allows you to set up custom instructions that enable you to provide the LLM with instructions about how you wish it to respond to your prompts. These custom instructions are applied to every prompt thereafter unless you ask for them to be disabled. You can also edit or delete the custom instructions.

The custom instructions feature enables you to share information with the chatbot about your personal preferences, such as the tone of the response or any limitations on the data to be used. You can also add information about yourself so that the outputs take into account the nature of your work and interests.

There are two parts to a custom instruction:

- The first part asks you to state, in less than 1,500 words, all that you would wish ChatGPT to know about you and the context in which you are asking for help.

- The second part enables you to instruct ChatGPT on how to respond when generating content. This includes your suggestions regarding the voice in which the outputs will be expressed, such as conversational, formal, or theatrical. You can also specify the tone to be used, such as encouraging, sombre, enthusiastic or critical. Finally, what style would you prefer — long or short sentences? Bulleted list? Table? Image?

Remember that once set up, you no longer need to include these details in your prompts when asking for content to be generated.

To access custom instructions, select Settings (bottom left screen icon of your account); then select 'Customize ChatGPT' from the list.

Example of enabling custom instructions

ChatGPT:
> What would you like ChatGPT to know about you to provide better responses?

You:
> I am a primary school teacher, teaching children aged 10 and 11. I will be following the Scottish Curriculum for Excellence. My aim is to develop these children's language and numeracy skills to the standards set out in the curriculum benchmarks and inculcate patterns of good behaviour, including respect and compassion. I also want to promote group work and collaboration. Your responses should take an intersectional approach.

ChatGPT:
> How would you like ChatGPT to respond?

You:
> Avoid long responses but provide enough detail to facilitate my understanding. Make your responses informal and suitable for 10–11-year-old children. Do not express opinions on topics—I need factual responses. Avoid overenthusiasm. Use bulleted lists to set out multi-part responses. Use simple analogies when explaining a concept, but avoid metaphors.

This instruction will be applied to all subsequent prompts, unless it is deleted or switched off. If all you want is a straightforward response from ChatGPT, you should switch off the custom instruction — it can be re-enabled later.

Develop your prompting skills

In addition to the suggestions from ChatGPT above, there are other ways to guide ChatGPT towards a response that will be valuable to you as a teacher and assessor in the classroom. You will encounter these as you work through the prompt exemplars given elsewhere in this book.
You can add the following requests to your prompts, if required:

- **Tone**: specify the tone that the LLM should adopt in its response (for example formal, professional, informative, persuasive, casual)
- **Format**: define how you wish the response to be presented to you (for example table, bulleted list, essay, dialogue, outline)
- **Acts as**: indicate a role or perspective that the LLM should adopt (for example critic, promoter, expert in a field)
- **Audience**: specify the target audience for tailored content
- **Language**: indicate the language, if you wish it to be different to the language in the prompt
- **Points of view**: ask the LLM to consider multiple perspectives or opinions
- **Counterarguments**: request that the response should address potential counterarguments
- **Sensitivity**: mention topics or issues that could be sensitive and should be handled with care, or avoided altogether

- **Analogies**: ask the LLM to use analogies or examples to clarify concepts

Using Generative AI to improve prompts

A good strategy to follow when generative AI responses are not hitting the mark is to ask the generative AI system to help you improve your prompt. For example, you might prompt ChatGPT in the following way:
> Act as an expert in writing LLM prompts. Consider the prompt below and provide helpful and specific feedback that would improve the prompt. Explain how this would be an improvement on the original. My Prompt: [add prompt here].

Replicating your voice

In the custom instruction, you may wish to find a way of guiding ChatGPT to adopt your particular 'voice' in its responses. This can be accomplished by providing ChatGPT with four or five pieces of content that you have created in your own style (without the use of AI) and asking ChatGPT to analyse this content in terms of its voice, tone, and style. You can then adjust ChatGPT's response and use this in the custom instruction.

If you have a favourite educator whose style and content you admire and wish to emulate, you can also do this exercise with content from that educator, taking care to observe intellectual property rights as you do so.

For example, here is what ChatGPT thinks of the material in this annex:

ChatGPT:

> The content provided outlines guidelines and considerations for the integration of Generative AI (GenAI) in educational settings. Here's an analysis of its voice, tone, and style:
>
> 1. Voice: The voice of this content is authoritative and informative. It speaks with the expertise of someone well-versed in the field of education and technology, likely aimed at educators and school administrators. The use of technical terms related to GenAI and references to specific legislation like GDPR or FERPA suggest a knowledgeable and professional voice.
>
> 2. Tone: The tone is cautionary and advisory, with a focus on responsible and ethical usage of GenAI in education. It balances the potential benefits of GenAI with warnings about its limitations and risks. Phrases like "be mindful", "ensure that", and "you should aim for a synergy" demonstrate a tone that is both instructive and precautionary.
>
> 3. Style: The style is formal and structured, with a clear division of topics into distinct sections. Each section begins with a heading, followed by explanatory text. The language is complex and academic, with long sentences and sophisticated vocabulary. The content is comprehensive, covering various aspects from the potential for over-reliance on technology to data privacy concerns and the risk of algorithmic bias.
>
> Overall, the content serves as a thorough guideline for educators, emphasizing careful and informed use of GenAI in educational settings. It seeks to educate and guide, ensuring that users are aware of both the capabilities and the limitations of such technology in the context of teaching and student relationships.

A good source of prompts can be found on GitHub[22].

---

[22] GitHub, Inc. (2024) *Prompts for Education: Enhancing Productivity & Learning*. Available at: https://github.com/microsoft/prompts-for-edu#prompts-for-education-enhancing-productivity--learning (Accessed March 2024).

We are providing updates on creating effective prompts on our blog —
AI Power in the Classroom (https://theaipoweredclassroom.org).

We welcome feedback on how we can improve teaching and learning with AI. Scan the QR Code with your phone to access the blog.

ANNEX 2 Curriculum and lesson planning

Curriculum planning

You can use AI to generate teaching and learning activities from curriculum descriptions and learning outcomes.

For example, a design and technology course has defined the following areas of learning to be explored at different stages in school:

'Understand the impact of product design and manufacture on the environment.'

AI can be used to generate specific learning outcomes and a range of possible learning activities for a specific stage. Using the Claude AI tool produced the following:

You:
> You are an expert teacher of Design and Technology. Suggest five key learning outcomes that Grade 8 students (13-year-olds) should achieve to show that they understand the following area of learning: 'Understand the impact of product design and manufacture on the environment.'
> And for each outcome suggest three key learning activities.

Claude:
> Here are five suggested key learning outcomes for 8th grade students to understand the impact of product design and manufacture on the environment, along with three key learning activities for each:
>
> Learning Outcome 1: Students will be able to identify the environmental impacts of different materials used in product design and manufacture.
>
> Activities:
> Compare the environmental costs and benefits of using wood, plastic, and metal for a sample product.

Research the life cycle environmental impacts from raw material extraction to disposal of several common manufactured product materials.
Class debate on the most environmentally sustainable materials for a new smartphone design.

Learning Outcome 2: Students will understand key strategies for reducing the environmental impact of product designs.

Activities:
Analyse sample products focused on sustainability and environmental impact reduction in their design.
Brainstorm ways to redesign everyday products to reduce their environmental impacts.
Design their own environmentally sustainable version of a common consumer product.

Learning Outcome 3: Students will be able to evaluate whether a product design properly incorporates end-of-life considerations.

Activities:
Take apart electronic or other consumer products and examine if they were designed for easy recycling or reuse.
Research manufacturer end-of-life product handling processes and compare against best practices.
Propose improved end-of-life product design solutions for real products that are environmentally problematic at their end of life.

Learning Outcome 4. Students will know best practices for sustainable and environmentally responsible manufacturing.

Activities:
Tour a local manufacturing facility focused on environmentally sustainable practices.
Compare and contrast traditional and sustainable manufacturing processes.
Research leading sustainably-focused product manufacturers and present to the class on their environmental initiatives.

Learning Outcome 5. Students will appreciate how consumer product choices impact sustainability.

Activities:
Self-evaluate daily product choices for sustainability impact.
Debate merits and downsides of different green product rating certifications and labels.
Campaign to educate friends and family on making environmentally sustainable consumer purchases.

You:

> This answers the question, but it is pitched too high for my students. Repeat the question, and, this time, produce answers which are not so demanding.

Claude:

> Got it, let me try simplifying the key learning outcomes and activities to be more accessible for grade 8 students:
>
> Learning Outcome 1: Students will know the difference between renewable and non-renewable materials used in products.
>
> Activities:
> Sort materials into renewable and non-renewable categories.
> Research the sources of common product materials (wood, plastic, metal, etc.).
> Discuss examples of sustainable renewable materials that could replace non-renewables.
>
> Learning Outcome 2: Students will recognize when product packaging is excessive or wasteful.
>
> Activities:
> Evaluate product packaging in the classroom for recyclability and necessity.
> Redesign product packaging to reduce waste.
> Debate pros and cons of plastic packaging versus alternatives.
>
> Learning Outcome 3: Students will consider product end-of-life when brainstorming designs.
>
> Activities:
> Take apart broken appliances and observe if they can be easily recycled.
> Research local recycling capabilities before selecting materials to use in a design project.
> Discuss ways everyday products could be redesigned to be more recycling-friendly.
>
> Learning Outcome 4: Students will know basic environmentally-friendly manufacturing practices.
>
> Activities:
> Watch videos on sustainability in manufacturing plants.
> Identify wasteful manufacturing practices that could be reduced.
> Research companies working to manufacture more sustainably.
>
> Learning Outcome 5: Students will reflect on recycling and reuse in their own lives.

> Activities:
> Self-audit of recycling habits at home.
> Discuss ways to reduce household waste related to products and packaging.
> Brainstorm creative ideas for reusing everyday product packaging and materials in art projects.
>
> How's that? I aimed for less complex outcomes and activities more feasible for 8th grade. Please let me know if the level still needs adjustment.

This example shows that you can obtain a more appropriate result by not accepting the first answer provided by generative AI systems.

At the time of writing, asking generative AI tools to recommend resources for learning and teaching is not always successful. You should compare the outputs from two or more AI tools. We can expect generative AI tools to improve in performance as they learn from prompts and responses related to curriculum design and lesson planning.

Lesson planning

AI can provide ideas for lesson planning. For example, in Scotland, a primary school teacher is expected to teach their children to achieve the following numeracy outcome:

'I can conduct simple experiments involving chance and communicate my predictions and findings using the vocabulary of probability.'

Here is a dialogue with ChatGPT to generate some ideas for individual lessons:

You:

> You are a primary school teacher, and you want your 10-year-old students to be able to achieve the following outcome:
> 'I can conduct simple experiments involving chance and communicate my predictions and findings using the vocabulary of probability.'
> Could you suggest three activities that my class can do to achieve this outcome and specify the resources that will be needed?
> The students will be working collaboratively in groups and each group will work on one activity.

ChatGPT:

> Certainly! Here are three activities that your 10-year-old students can do to achieve the outcome of conducting simple experiments involving chance and communicating their predictions and findings using the vocabulary of probability. Each activity is designed to be done collaboratively in groups, and I'll also suggest the resources needed for each activity:
>
> 1. **Coin Toss Experiment:**
> Resources: Coins (preferably different denominations), a chart for recording results.
> Activity: Each group can flip a coin multiple times and record whether it lands on heads or tails. They can discuss and make predictions about the outcomes. Then, they can calculate and discuss the probability of getting heads or tails based on their results.
>
> 2. **Dice Roll Experiment:**
> Resources: Dice, recording sheets, and coloured markers.
> Activity: Groups can roll a standard six-sided dice and record the numbers rolled. They can discuss their predictions and calculate the probability of rolling each number. Additionally, they can compare the outcomes when rolling multiple dice to understand the concept of probability distribution.
>
> 3. **Spinner Probability:**
> Resources: Spinners with different sectors, recording sheets, coloured markers.
> Activity: Each group can create or use spinners with different colours or numbers on the sectors. They can predict and record which sector the spinner lands on after multiple spins. Then, they can calculate and discuss the probability of landing on each sector.
>
> For each activity, encourage students to communicate their predictions and findings using probability vocabulary such as "likely,"

"unlikely," "certain," "impossible," "probability," and fractions or percentages when appropriate. Also, facilitate group discussions where they can share their results and conclusions with their classmates.

This is a reasonable response. To save time, you could ask ChatGPT to print instructions for each activity because you intend to use them in a carousel to enable the children to experience all of the activities in turn. You could also ask for a series of graded questions for the students to answer on a card.

You:
>Thank you. For each of these three activities, could you please print clear instructions for the students to enable them to carry out the activities in simple language, in numbered steps? Also, could you give me four questions for each activity for the students to answer to check what they have learned from the activity? The questions should check their use of the language of probability. The four questions should be graded. The first question should be easy, and the questions should be progressively more difficult, from question 1 to question 2 to question 3 to question 4.

ChatGPT:
>Certainly! Here are clear instructions in simple language with numbered steps for each of the six activities, along with four graded questions for each activity to check the students' understanding of the language of probability:
>
>**Activity 1: Coin Toss Experiment**
>
>**Instructions:**
>1. Each group gets a coin and a chart.
>2. Decide who will flip the coin first.
>3. The flipper tosses the coin in the air and catches it.
>4. Record if it lands on heads (H) or tails (T) on the chart.
>5. Do this 10 times.
>6. Talk about what you noticed.
>7. Now, predict if it will be heads or tails on the next flip.
>8. After everyone predicts, flip the coin again and see if your predictions were right.

Questions:
1. What did you see more of, heads or tails? (easy)
2. How many times did it land on heads out of 10 flips? (moderate)
3. What do you think is the chance of getting heads on the next flip? (challenging)
4. If you flipped the coin 20 more times, how many times do you think it will land on heads? (difficult)

Activity 2: Dice Roll Experiment

Instructions:
1. Each group gets a dice and recording sheets.
2. Take turns rolling the dice.
3. Record the number that shows up each time.
4. Roll the dice 20 times.
5. Discuss which numbers came up more often.
6. Predict what number will come up next.
7. Roll the dice again to check your prediction.

Questions:
1. What number did you roll the most times? (easy)
2. How many different numbers did you roll? (moderate)
3. What's the chance of rolling a 6 on the next roll? (challenging)
4. If you rolled the dice 50 more times, how many times do you think you'll get a 3? (difficult)

Activity 3: Spinner Probability

Instructions:
1. Each group gets a spinner and recording sheets.
2. Spin the spinner 15 times.
3. Record which colour or number it lands on each time.
4. Talk about which colours or numbers appeared most.
5. Predict what it will land on next.
6. Spin the spinner again to see if you're right.

Questions:
1. Which colour or number did the spinner land on the most? (easy)
2. How many different colours or numbers did you get? (moderate)
3. What's the chance of landing on blue on the next spin? (challenging)
4. If you spun the spinner 30 more times, how many times do you think it will land on green? (difficult)

These instructions and questions are designed to progressively challenge students' understanding of probability while using

> appropriate language. You can adjust the number of trials or spins based on your students' needs and the time available for each activity.

This is a reasonable first draft that the teacher could print or modify. A more sophisticated response could be obtained by providing a class template for the AI tool to populate.

ANNEX 3 Developing rubrics

Many teachers find that developing and using rubrics helps students to assess and improve their work standards. The following is an example of how to develop a rubric using Claude to help senior students improve the quality of their presentations to their classmates.

You:
> You are an expert teacher of senior school students aged 16 to 18. State seven criteria that can be used to judge the quality of an oral presentation given by one of your students.

Claude:
> Here are 7 criteria I would use as an expert teacher to judge the quality of an oral presentation given by a senior school student aged 16-18 years old:
>
> 1. Organization: Does the presentation have a clear introduction, logical flow between main points, and an effective conclusion? Is the information presented in a structured way that is easy to follow?
>
> 2. Engagement: Does the presenter make eye contact, vary tone and pace, and use gestures to fully engage the audience? Do they draw in listeners and keep their attention?
>
> 3. Content: Is the information presented accurate, relevant to the topic, and at the right level for the audience? Is there enough depth and quality of information?
>
> 4. Visual Aids: Do visual aids enhance the presentation rather than distract? Are they easy to see, read, and interpret? Do they highlight key points?
>
> 5. Delivery: Does the presenter speak clearly, avoid filler words, project their voice well, and speak at an appropriate pace? Do they sound polished and prepared?
>
> 6. Discussion: Does the presenter effectively address questions and feedback about the topic? Do they demonstrate knowledge and the ability to have a meaningful exchange?

7. Timeliness: Does the presenter stay within the allotted time? Do they manage time properly to cover content without rushing or dragging?

These are acceptable standards, and we now need them in a table along with levels of achievement.

You:
> Produce a Rubric in a table with these seven standards, abbreviated to one word for each standard; for example Organisation for the first standard.
> Each standard is to be judged at four levels of achievement.
> Provide the rubric with appropriate standards for each criterion for each of the four levels.

Claude:
> Here is a rubric table with the 7 standards abbreviated to one word and described at four levels of achievement:

Standard	Exceeds Expectations (4)	Meets Expectations (3)	Approaching Expectations (2)	Fails to Meet Expectations (1)
Organisation	Highly structured, easy to follow, seamless flow	Clear structure and flow	Attempts structure but sometimes confusing	No clear structure or flow
Engagement	Fully engages audience with eye contact, varied tone, and gestures	Consistent eye contact and engagement techniques	Some engagement but inconsistent	Little eye contact or audience engagement
Content	Accurate, in-depth information at a high level	Accurate, relevant info at appropriate level	Mostly accurate but lacks depth	Significant inaccuracies or irrelevant info
Visual Aids	Great visuals provide clarity, emphasis & interest	Aids are readable, interpretable, well-incorporated	Visual aids used but may be difficult to interpret	Minimal, confusing visual aids
Delivery	Crisp and polished with excellent pacing and clarity	Clear delivery and appropriate pacing	Delivery could be more crisp and polished	Lacking clarity, difficult to understand
Discussion	Insightful, direct responses advancing understanding	Capably addresses questions and feedback	Superficially responds to questions and feedback	Unable to meaningfully discuss and respond
Timeliness	Finishes presentation within allotted time	Stays within allotted time	Portions rushed/dragged due to time mismanagement	Significantly too long or short

This is a credible rubric that the teacher could use to help their students judge their peers' presentations and provide constructive feedback. Alternatively, the teacher could give this rubric to their students and ask them to work with a peer and use the rubric to help them prepare and deliver their individual presentations.

The presentation of instructions and information in a well-organised and logical fashion, with examples to improve the clarity of communication as in this example, helps to improve the reliability of the AI tools responses and minimises hallucinations.

ANNEX 4 Assessments and quizzes

You can readily use AI to construct quizzes, homework exercises and end-of-unit assessments. AI can help you to construct quizzes that require students to provide a single answer, or they can include multiple-choice items, where students have to select the correct answer.

Here is a simple lesson quiz, following an introductory lesson on cell biology.

You:
>As an expert biology teacher, you will produce an exit quiz based on an introductory cell structure biology lesson.
>The lesson has the following content:
>'Cell ultrastructure and functions — cell wall, mitochondrion, chloroplast, cell membrane, cytoplasm, vacuole, nucleus, ribosome and plasmid using examples from typical plant, animal, fungal and bacterial cells.'
>Produce a quiz with five questions based on this lesson's content.

Claude:
>Here is a 5-question quiz on cell structure and functions:
>
>1. Which of the following organelles is found in plant cells but not animal cells?
>a) Mitochondria
>b) Cell wall
>c) Nucleus
>d) Ribosomes

2. Chloroplasts are organelles that contain chlorophyll pigments and conduct photosynthesis. In which type of cell would you expect to find them?
a) Bacterial cells
b) Fungal cells
c) Plant cells
d) Animal cells

3. Which organelle is responsible for breaking down and digesting macromolecules?
a) Lysosome
b) Golgi apparatus
c) Endoplasmic reticulum
d) Vacuole

4. The cell membrane is composed primarily of _____.
a) Phospholipids
b) Cellulose
c) Chitin
d) Peptidoglycan

5. Which of the following is NOT a component of the cytoplasm?
a) Cytosol
b) Organelles
c) Inclusions
d) Cell wall

This is a credible first draft that the teacher can adapt to their own class.

ANNEX 5 Data analysis

LLMs can analyse students' performance data. A spreadsheet file can be pasted in or attached to an AI dialogue box, and you can then ask it questions about the data. The following example was created to illustrate this.

A spreadsheet was constructed for 20 students who had 10 end-of-unit assessments; the average score obtained for the class on each assessment and the total marks gained by each student were provided. The spreadsheet was then attached to the dialogue box.

You:
> This is a spreadsheet of student Grades and Unit assessments. It includes each student's Total score and the Average score achieved by all students in each unit assessment.
> Provide a high-level analysis of this data.

GPT 4:
> Here is a high-level analysis of the student performance data from the spreadsheet:
>
> **Average Scores per Unit**:
> Unit 1: 63.80
> Unit 2: 66.05
> Unit 3: 65.65
> Unit 4: 57.90
> Unit 5: 61.55
> Unit 6: 55.65
> Unit 7: 68.25
> Unit 8: 62.50
> Unit 9: 48.70
> Unit 10: 62.95
>
> **Overall Average Total Score Across All Units**: 613.0
>
> **Highest and Lowest Scoring Units**:
> The highest scoring unit is Unit 7, with an average score of 68.25.
> The lowest scoring unit is Unit 9, with an average score of 48.70.

Total Scores:
  The highest total score achieved by a student is 736.0.
  The lowest total score achieved by a student is 529.0.

This analysis suggests that students performed best on Unit 7, while Unit 9 was the most challenging. The overall average score indicates a moderately high level of performance across all units.

Further analyses can be obtained by asking follow-up questions.

You:
   The unit 1 assessments took place before the unit 10 assessments. Are there any significant trends in the performance data? Are any students improving their performance? Are any students performing less well in later assessments?

GPT4:
   Based on the performance data from Unit 1 to Unit 10 assessments, the following trends are observed:

   Students with Improved Performance: 8 students showed an improvement in their scores from Unit 1 to Unit 10.
   Students with Declined Performance: 12 students experienced a decline in their scores from Unit 1 to Unit 10.

   The score differences between Unit 1 and Unit 10 for each student reveal a mixed trend. While a notable number of students improved their scores, a slightly higher number of students showed a decline in performance in the later assessment (Unit 10) compared to the initial assessment (Unit 1).

   This suggests that while some students have adapted and improved over time, a larger group found the later material more challenging, or perhaps other factors affected their performance.

Using an AI tool can provide an overview of data. However, you should exercise caution in using this approach with LLMs as they can readily hallucinate. It is important that you structure data and prompts logically, to reduce this possibility.

ANNEX 6 Reporting: enhancing teacher-parent communication

As discussed earlier, AI tools can summarise data and spot trends. Therefore, they can be used to analyse individual student performance across the curriculum. Such analyses can be combined to produce a detailed report on a student and include other information, such as attendance, participation in extracurricular activities, and other achievements. This facility should save personal tutors and class teachers a great deal of time.

In today's rapidly evolving educational landscape, effective teacher-parent communication is paramount. One essential aspect of this communication is the timely and informative reporting of a student's progress. AI-powered tools enable you to streamline the report-writing process, as well as making it more efficient and insightful.

The AI toolset available for report writing includes generative AI tools, such as ChatGPT, and products created for this specific purpose, such as Real Fast Reports.[23] This latter tool is tailored specifically for teachers seeking to create student reports quickly and efficiently. Generative AI, on the other hand, offers versatile applications, including report writing. These tools allow you to dedicate more time to providing meaningful feedback to your students without the burden of report composition.

Despite the rise of digital communication, traditional school reports remain a cornerstone for conveying a young person's progress toward becoming a responsible adult. In today's fast-paced world, parents may

---

[23] Real Fast Reports. Available at: https://realfastreports.com/ (Accessed March 2024).

find it challenging to attend every parent-teacher meeting throughout the year. Hence, a well-written end-of-term report becomes indispensable, giving parents essential insights into their child's academic journey and a chance to celebrate their achievements.

While the idea of AI automating report generation is tempting, it's essential to remember that no one knows the students better than you as their teacher. Teachers must be pivotal in report writing to ensure the reports feel personal and individualised. Generic reports hold little value for parents, who seek reports that resonate with their child's unique journey. Generative AI can facilitate this process, making it faster and easier while maintaining the personal touch.

The evolution of report writing from handwritten notes to digital formats marked a significant leap in school administration. AI now offers the potential to make another significant advance by transforming student information from concise bullet points into clear and informative prose. The result is that each report is individualised and aligned with the teacher's assessments, with the time required for composition significantly reduced.

The benefits of AI for teachers when writing reports are multifaceted. AI excels at producing grammatically correct content that is free from spelling errors. It can adapt language to suit the intended purpose, allowing teachers to focus on the substance of their reports rather than the writing process. This reduces the likelihood of typing errors and enables the re-use of appropriate content, further streamlining the report-writing process. Ultimately, AI enables reports to remain meaningful, while reducing the input required from teachers, promoting their wellbeing and reducing stress.

If you're interested in exploring AI report-writing platforms, you'll find a growing number of options available. Beyond Real Fast Reports, which is specifically designed for school report writing, various AI-powered tools cater to different educational needs. Schools should consider piloting AI-based reporting, to unlock its potential benefits and enhance teacher-parent communication.

Here is an example of how you might start:

Prompt:

> < You have extensive knowledge of the use of AI in helping teachers to write end-of-term reports for their students. Provide three different examples of how this might work in practice. Explain what information the teachers need to provide and what the form of the output would be. >

ChatGPT:

> Here are three different examples of how AI can assist teachers in writing end-of-term reports for their students, along with the required input information and the form of the output:
>
> AI-Generated Descriptive Reports:
>
> Input Information: The teacher provides essential student data, including their name, grade, subjects, and assessments. Additionally, the teacher can input specific achievements, areas of improvement, behaviour observations, and any personalised comments they wish to include.
>
> Output Form: The AI generates comprehensive, personalised, and well-structured descriptive reports for each student. These reports typically include an introductory paragraph, sections on academic performance in various subjects, extracurricular activities, behaviour, and comments. The output can be in a printable PDF format or a digital document that can be shared with parents.

Summarised Insights Reports:

Input Information: Teachers input key performance data, such as test scores, assignment grades, attendance records, and participation levels for each student. The teacher may also provide their own observations and comments.

Output Form: The AI compiles the input data and generates summarised insights reports. These reports may include charts, graphs, and visual representations of student performance trends. They provide a quick overview of a student's progress, highlighting areas of strength and areas requiring improvement. The output can be in a visually appealing format, such as a dashboard, suitable for online viewing or printing.

Customised Template-Based Reports:

Input Information: The teacher selects from predefined templates or formats for the report, specifying the sections they want to include (e.g., academic achievements, behaviour, extracurricular activities). They then input student-specific data, such as grades, attendance, and notable accomplishments.

Output Form: The AI populates the selected template with the provided information, creating customised reports. Teachers can further personalise these reports by adding specific comments or anecdotes for each student. The output can be in various formats, including Word documents or editable templates, allowing teachers to make final adjustments before sharing them with parents.

In all these examples, AI assists teachers by automating the time-consuming process of report creation, allowing them to focus more on analysing student performance and providing meaningful insights.

ANNEX 7 Research

AI tools can save teachers a lot of time on research-based activities. They can be used to:

- summarise research and government policy papers
- compare different policy papers and identify common areas and those that are different
- organise information and data differently by restructuring and printing tables in different formats
- develop presentations based on policy papers and research reports
- generate ideas for research and suggest the structure for reports
- edit reports and adjust the tone, grammar and expression

Here is a simple example of AI reorganising information. The following was the published membership of a Scottish Policy Group, organised alphabetically by surname:

> Billy Burke Head Teacher, Renfrew High School
> Professor Graham Donaldson, University of Glasgow
> Professor Louise Hayward, University of Glasgow
> Professor Walter Humes, University of Stirling
> Professor Anne Looney, Dublin City University
> Khadija Mohammed, University of the West of Scotland/Scottish Association of Minority Ethnic Educators
> Cathy McCulloch, Children's Parliament
> Dr Naomi Stanford, Naomi Stanford Organisation Design

This can be presented in a table as follows:

You:
> Present the following information in a table.
> <Copy and paste the text into the dialogue box>

Claude:
> Here is the information presented in a table with the requested column names:
>
> | Name | Organisation |
> |---|---|
> | Billy Burke | Head Teacher, Renfrew High School |
> | Professor Graham Donaldson | University of Glasgow |
> | Professor Louise Hayward | University of Glasgow |
> | Professor Walter Humes | University of Stirling |
> | Professor Anne Looney | Dublin City University |
> | Khadija Mohammed | University of the West of Scotland/Scottish Association of Minority Ethnic Educators |
> | Cathy McCulloch | Children's Parliament |
> | Dr Naomi Stanford | Naomi Stanford Organisation Design |

You:
> Reorganise this table by making the first column the Organisation organised alphabetically and the second column the relevant Name.

Claude:
> Here is the table with the columns swapped and rows organized alphabetically by Organisation:

Organisation	Name
Children's Parliament	Cathy McCulloch
Dublin City University	Professor Anne Looney
Head Teacher, Renfrew High School	Billy Burke
Naomi Stanford Organisation Design	Dr Naomi Stanford
Scottish Association of Minority Ethnic Educators /University of the West of Scotland	Khadija Mohammed
University of Glasgow	Professor Graham Donaldson
University of Glasgow	Professor Louise Hayward
University of Stirling	Professor Walter Humes

This simple task can readily be done with Microsoft Excel or Word, but sometimes it is quicker to use an AI tool to reorganise information.

ANNEX 8 Generative AI prompts by topic

In the 'AI across the curriculum' chapter, we present an overview of how individual subjects (English, Mathematics, Science, etc) could use generative AI to reduce teacher workload, create resources (including lesson plans and assessments) and provide support for students.

In Annex 1, we show how to generate effective prompts by their using current generative AI tools. Annexes 2 to 7 provide detailed examples of the various types of generative AI responses that can be obtained through prompting.

This Annex provides further details on each type of generative AI response for the following topics in the curriculum. The examples are selected from several different educational jurisdictions, to demonstrate the ubiquity of these AI tools.

- English and literacy
- Mathematics and numeracy
- Science
- Languages
- Social Studies and Humanities
- Expressive Arts and Music
- Design, Technology and Computing
- Health and Wellbeing

English and literacy
Here are further examples of prompts that could be useful to you as a teacher of English and literacy.

An example of a prompt to produce a **writing assignment** for a class:

> <You are an expert in creating exercises for writing assignments in an English language curriculum.
> My 9th grade class are studying the novella Of Mice and Men by John Steinbeck.
> Create a writing assignment to be completed in class by my students.
> The assignment should take 35–40 minutes to complete.
> It should prompt the students to write about particular characters, themes or symbols in the novella.>

An example of a prompt to produce a **creative writing assignment** for a class:

> <Your expertise includes understanding the key elements that contribute to creative writing, such as narrative voice, character development, evocative setting and pace.
> I want to set my Year 11 class a creative writing assignment in which they are reporting an event from the Boston Tea Party incident in 1773. Their writing should reflect colonist and British viewpoints and include human interest elements.
> Create an assignment brief for my class and include source references for this incident.
> The assignment should take no more than 2 hours of writing to complete.>

Your students could also make use of generative AI to help them understand topics. Here is an example that you can try for yourself.

Here is an example of a **help me understand** prompt that a student could use:

> <I am a student in a 10th Grade class. I have some difficulty understanding the themes that are present in a Shakespeare play. I am studying Hamlet.

> In particular, I want to understand how Hamlet's constant anxiety about the difference between appearance and reality is represented in Act 1 Scene 4.
> Ask me some questions to establish the extent of my present understanding.
> Then help me fill in the gaps in my understanding of Hamlet's anxiety in this scene.>

As outlined in earlier sections of this book, generative AI can help you manage your workload by generating lesson plans, marking schemes and even answers to the most frequently asked questions (FAQs).

Here is an example of a prompt that creates an individual **lesson plan**:

> <You are an expert in creating lessons that engage high school students in the study of literacy as set out in the curriculum for Key Stage 3 in England.
> Help me create a 40-minute lesson that addresses the following curricular requirement:
> 'Understand how the work of dramatists is communicated effectively through performance and how alternative staging allows for different interpretations of a play.'
> This lesson is for Year 9 and should be teacher-led. Suggest a suitable drama that I can use to illustrate the concepts.
> Give me the learning objectives, a step-by-step breakdown of activities, and an exit ticket.>

Here is an example of a prompt that produces a **resource** for teaching:

> <You are an expert in the curriculum for the GCE in English Language. I want to guide students in a Year 11 class to adopt a systematic approach to reviewing essay work produced by other class members. An essay can either be a piece of creative writing or a discursive essay. Provide a template for each type that the students can follow in the review process.>

Here is an example of a prompt to suggest **teaching and learning approaches**:

<You have a comprehensive understanding of English language development in young children. My class of 8-year-olds is struggling with cursive writing. Suggest approaches and exercises that I can use that will give them the competence to improve and the motivation to do so.>

In using prompts like the above, remember that you can (and should!) always ask generative AI tools to improve its response, either by providing additional information (such as educational level) or just asking it to do better. Used ethically, such generative AI literacy tools increase differentiation, engagement and agency, while building core skills.

Mathematics and numeracy

Here is an example of a prompt to create an **assignment** for a high school mathematics class studying statistics:

> <You are a well experienced teacher of maths to GCSE level in the UK. You have particular expertise in designing learning experiences that promote concept-driven enquiry learning. Create an assignment for a class studying at Key Stage 4 level in the UK that requires them to create and interpret a box-plot from data. The assignment should require each student to find or generate their own dataset. Between 40 and 60 data items are required.>

Here is an example of a prompt for **lesson planning** in early years mathematics:

> <You are expert in the effective teaching of maths topics to pupils in their early years of school. You know how to motivate and inspire them and help them to enjoy maths. You have a sound knowledge of the maths curriculum set out by the NCCA in Ireland.
> Create an outline plan for series of six lessons of 1 hour duration each on Shape and Space from the NCCA curriculum. My aim is to promote agency and self-efficacy in my pupils.>

Here is an example of a prompt to create **assessments** in a mathematics topic:

> <Formative assessment is an important element in the development of mathematical understanding and reasoning. You are expert in the creation of formative assessments in maths that support learning of the topic: Ratios and Proportions.
> Create a set of six formative assessment activities on this topic that would be suitable for pupils aged 15 years who are following the International Baccalaureate curriculum. For each assessment indicate its level of difficulty, the concept that is being tested and any likely misconceptions on the part of students.>

Here is an example of a **help me understand** prompt that a student could use:

> <I need help with understanding how to read Roman numerals that show a particular year. I find the order of the symbols difficult to remember. I am in Year 5 at a school in Wales. Can you give me a step-by-step way of reading a year date as a Roman numeral?>

Here is an example of a prompt that creates a set of **resources** for mathematics teaching:

> <Help me create a set of maths resources to support me in my teaching of the topic of trigonometry following the Scottish Curriculum for Excellence at National 5 level. My style of teaching favours inquiry-based learning. When creating resources, take into account differentiation. I also want students to understand applications of trigonometry in the real world and to use physical manipulatives.>

These examples demonstrate the kind of prompts that you can use to support your work as a mathematics teacher and help your students in their learning and comprehension of mathematics. As before, it is worthwhile ensuring that you provide the generative AI tool with sufficient information to help it focus its responses. Asking the generative AI tool to improve its response, either with or without additional information from you, is always a good strategy.

Languages

Generative AI lends itself well to helping teachers create learning resources that are pitched at a given level of language competence in students.

Here is an example of a prompt to create class **activities** that can help build vocabulary:

> <You have an expert understanding of the challenges that young people face in learning another language. Suggest some inquiry-based activities that can help
> 16-year-old students in Canada with basic Spanish proficiency build their vocabulary in a fun and engaging way. At least one of these should be a collaborative activity.>

Here is an example of a prompt to create **activities** that can help build speaking confidence:

> <You have expert knowledge of best practices in language learning in school education. Suggest engaging role-playing scenarios that would encourage GCSE Year 2 French language learners in the UK to practise speaking confidently in a variety of everyday situations.>

Here is an example of a prompt to create **resources** that can be used for grammar development:

> <Create some interactive grammar games that will make practising specific grammar structures in German both fun and effective for 15-year-old learners in an
> English-speaking country.>

Here is an example of a **help me understand** prompt that a student could use:

> <You have a good understanding of the language curriculum requirements at A level in the UK. I am studying Italian and have chosen the novel "Il Giorno Della Civetta" by Leonardo Sciascia as my text for this course. Help me understand the following: (a) how the characters play out the central themes of the novel; and (b) the key moral or ethical dilemma in the plot. Draw on some phrases or sentences from the novel to help me relate the Italian text to your suggested answer.>

You can harness generative AI's remarkable ability to translate between multiple languages to produce learning materials and other resources at a level consistent with the student's level of ability.

Science

The teaching of science subjects is another fertile ground for generative AI, with its ability to suggest practical lab-based activities linked to science concepts and create formative assessments that are differentiated.

Here is an example of a prompt to generate a small group **assignment**:

> <You have expertise in the design of practical activities in a high school context that help students learn concepts in Chemistry. A Year 10 class is following the English National Curriculum in Chemistry. Generate an assignment that requires students to work in small groups to identify three metals. Students will have 40 minutes to complete this assignment.
> Specify the materials I should provide, the safety precautions I should take and a step-by-step procedure guide for the assignment. Provide a marking guide.>

Here is an example of a prompt to generate **a plan for a topic:**

> <You are experienced in designing and structuring learning activities that help children understand science concepts. I want to engage a Year 5 class (Key Stage 2) with the following curriculum aim: 'Describe the differences in the life cycles of a mammal, an amphibian, an insect and a bird.'
> Suggest a series of class activities that would lead to students achieving this aim. Make the activities purposeful and engaging for this age of student. For each activity state the objective in the learning.>

Here is an example of a prompt to generate **assessments:**

> <A S3 (third-year) class in a Scottish secondary school has studied the topic of fractional distillation of crude oil as per the Scottish Curriculum for Excellence for Science level 4. The national benchmark expects students to identify and describe the importance of at least three everyday substances that are made from hydrocarbons.

> Create a multiple-choice quiz that test both factual knowledge and conceptual understanding of this topic. Provide the correct answer and ensure that the distractors in each question would be plausible to students at this age and stage.>

Here is an example of a **help me understand** prompt that a student could use:

> <I am studying Earth and Space Science in a Grade 12 high school in Ontario. I am finding difficulty with this particular aspect of my studies: 'Identify and describe the various methods of isotopic age determination, giving for each the name of the isotope, its half-life, its effective dating range, and some of the materials that it can be used to date.' Create a series of resources for me that will lead me step-by-step to reach an understanding of this important topic. Create a test in the form of a quiz that will check my understanding.>

Generative AI science tools can inspire curiosity and scientific thinking through interactive discovery. Conversational generative AI is a very effective tool to help students gain an understanding of science topics at their own pace.

Social Studies and Humanities

Generative AI can effectively support you in creating learning activities that help foster understanding in subjects such as Citizenship, Sociology, and Psychology. This type of AI excels in its knowledge of historical events. However, you should not expect generative AI to have a knowledge of more recent world events, as these models are trained on largely historical data.

Here is an example of a prompt that creates a **lesson plan:**

> <You have expert knowledge of sustainability issues and how to exemplify them for young students. I am teaching a Grade 7 class in Ontario. My topic for the next few lessons is natural resource extraction/harvesting and use in some specific regions of the world. Create a lesson plan aligned to the Ontario school curriculum suited to this age group and focusing on the sustainability of the processes to be covered in my topic.>

Here is an example of a prompt that creates an **assignment** for students:

> <You are an experienced teacher of Sociology to young students. You know how to create assignments that engage and motivate students and promote interaction in their learning. I am teaching GCSE Sociology in an international school in the UAE and need your help to suggest an assignment for my class that will help them understand the 'differing views of the functions of families' as per the GCSE Sociology curriculum. Provide a prompt sheet for the students. Provide me with an explanation of the purpose of the assignment and how it links to this curriculum topic. Create a marking rubric for the assignment.>

Here is an example of a prompt that creates an **assessment:**

> <You understand how to create high-quality multiple-choice questions (MCQs) that provide a scenario and include plausible distractors. I want your help to create a set of high quality MCQs for my 16-year-old students who are studying the Scottish National 5 curriculum in History.
> The MCQs should test students' understanding of the economic, political, religious and legal effects of the Treaty of Union 1707. Provide answers and explain how they relate to this curriculum topic.>

Here is an example of a prompt that creates **classroom activities** to enhance learning:

> <I am teaching GCSE Citizenship to Year 10 pupils in a UK school. My next topic is the process of parliamentary debate and deliberation of public issues as part of the process of making and shaping policy and legislation.
> You have expertise in creating fun and interactive classroom activities that will enhance learning. Use this expertise to suggest a set of classroom activities that will help my students to understand this topic. For each activity provide a statement of how it relates to the curriculum topic, the concept/concepts to be learned, and instructions for my students to follow.>

Here is an example of a **help me understand** prompt that a student could use:

> <I am studying the International Baccalaureate Diploma Programme (Higher level). I am struggling to understand the significance and impact of the London Naval Conference (1930) on global disarmament. I need your help. Explain to me the key outcomes from the conference, the main countries involved and how it influenced

> global disarmament at that time and in the future. Ask me questions to test my understanding. When you think I am ready, give me a final test with feedback on my answers.>

Here is an example of a prompt that would create a **resource** for use in a history context:

> <An activity that my students enjoy is to research a historical figure and build a profile that they then present to the rest of the class. I want to give the students a template that they can use when building the profile. It should enable them to make an interesting and engaging presentation of their historical figure. Create a template that can be used by Year 9 students (14-year-olds) for this purpose. As an example, populate the template with a profile of a figure from early Elizabethan era.>

Here is an example of a prompt that would create a **resource** for use in a geography context:

> <My Grade 6 class in the USA is learning about volcanoes and have been shown a set of well-known volcanoes of different types around the world. Generate instructions to help me create a set of flashcards suitable for revision of this topic. Each card should have an image of a volcano on the front and its type on the reverse side. The set of volcanoes should include at least three of each type.>

Expressive Arts and Music

Generative AI can create customised exercises for music practice, provide step-by-step guidance on instrument playing techniques, and assist in composing melodies, harmonies and rhythms. It can also emulate the styles of artists and art movements, to provide students with a broad spectrum of visual references.

Here is an example of a prompt that creates a **lesson plan:**

> <Create a detailed lesson plan focused on the basic concepts of harmony as set out in the K-12 Music curriculum for Grade 6 students. It should be designed to fit a 45-minute class period and cater to a diverse range of learning styles and abilities.
> The plan should state the objectives of the lesson, the theory component to be covered, the main activities and corresponding resources, and a suggested differentiation strategy for the lesson.>

Here is an example of a prompt that creates an **assignment** for students:

> <You have expertise in the teaching of art history to young people so that it is engaging and motivating. At Key Stage 3 in the UK curriculum my students (aged 14 years) are expected to know about great artists and understand the historical and cultural development of their art forms. Create an assignment for my students that would enable them to demonstrate their level of competence in this topic. They will have a period of 4 weeks to work on this in class and as homework. Provide a brief for the assignment along with step-by-step instructions. Provide me with an explanation of how the assignment satisfies the curriculum requirement and a scoring rubric for student submissions.>

Here is an example of a prompt that creates an **assessment**:

> <As a primary school teacher, I don't have a lot of confidence in delivering the Music element of the Scottish Curriculum for Excellence. My Level 4 class of 12-year-olds are required to demonstrate that they can 'listen to a wide range of music and identify and analyse technical aspects'. Create a suitable assessment appropriate to this age and stage that would help me assess how well the students perform on this criterion. Explain how your suggested assessment fits with the requirements of this curriculum and provide me with a scoring rubric.>

Note: The ChatGPT response to the above prompt suggested the creation and maintenance of a 'musical explorers journal' over the term.

Here is an example of a prompt that creates **classroom activities** to enhance learning:

> <You are expert in teaching the subject of Drama to teenage students and have a repertoire of ways to engage and motivate them in the study and performance of drama. My GCSE Drama students (mid-teens) should 'develop a range of theatrical skills and apply them to create performances'. Create classroom activities that would contribute to this course aim. For each activity, indicate its purpose and its level of difficulty and provide step by step instructions for students. Resource requirements should be stated.>

Here is an example of a **help me understand** prompt that a student could use:

> <In my music course at school I am having difficulty understanding the difference between ostinato and riff. They seem very similar to me when I hear them in a performance. I am in my first year of high school and I want to get my problem fixed for further my study of music. Can you take me through this very slowly — one step at a

time. It would help me if you could show me examples of each of these musical forms.>

Design, Technology and Computing

Here is an example of a prompt that creates a **lesson plan:**

> <Familiarise yourself with Alberta Education's Computer Science CSE1010 course. Prepare a lesson plan that will help me explain how the von Neumann architecture works and illustrate the data flows in the system. The lesson duration will be 40 minutes. Suggest follow-up activities for students to work on in their own time that would help ensure students grasp the fundamental concepts and can visualise the data flow within a computer system. Tell me of any visual resources I might require and where to source them in Canada.>

Here is an example of a prompt that creates an **assignment** for students:

> <I teach a course in Design and Manufacture at National 5 level to a class of 16-year-olds in Scotland. I am concerned that the students in this class are losing interest in their chosen qualification. My aim is to create an assignment that would increase their motivation to progress in this course. The students have covered research and idea generation for a sustainable product. My next topic is how to apply a range of modelling techniques to develop a design proposal. Create an assignment that focuses on the modelling phase, including instructions for the students to follow over a period of 2 weeks. Provide me with a rubric for assessing the quality of the submissions.>

Here is an example of a prompt that creates an **assessment:**

> <My students have been studying the topic of structures in their Irish Leaving Certificate Technology course. I wish to assess their knowledge and understanding of the differences between arch, shell, frame, beam and box structures and their ability to sketch them. I also wish to test their grasp of the effects of forces such as tension,

shear, compression, torsion and bending. Create an assessment that would cover these aspects of the syllabus at ordinary level. It should take no more than a 40-minute period to complete. Supply answers to aid my marking.>

Here is an example of a prompt that creates **classroom activities** to enhance learning:

<My A-level Computing students usually design and build software to a well-specified problem. I would like to expose them to the real-life process of eliciting requirements directly from a client. This usually takes the form of a question-and-answer interview with the client. I want you to act as the client for a software product that would solve the following problem. A tennis club allows members to book a court for a match. At the end of each month the club secretary reserves courts for club matches and then releases the available slots for members. He wants to know whether matches booked are singles or doubles and to find out who the most frequent users are. Do not provide all the information at once but respond only to the students' questions about the software requirement.>

Here is an example of a **help me understand** prompt that a student could use:

<I am a Year 9 student in a school in Wales, studying in the Science and Technology area. I am learning about codes and ciphers in cyber security and I am having difficulty understanding encryption and decryption as a means of securing data. Ask me some questions to see what I already know. Use my answers to correct any errors and then help me understand how encryption works in the simplest of terms. Ask some questions to check my understanding at the end of your explanation.>

Health and Wellbeing

Generative AI can be a powerful ally when you are planning and delivering health and wellbeing courses in a school setting. It can create lesson plans on themes such as stress management, healthy eating, sleep hygiene, body image, social media awareness, and coping with academic pressures. Generative AI can suggest engaging and interactive activities that cater to different learning styles and promote active participation.

Generative AI can curate accurate and up-to-date information from various sources, including research papers, health organisations, and educational resources. This helps to ensure your courses are based on reliable and evidence-based practices.

Health and Wellbeing topics demand consideration of cultural sensitivities and diverse backgrounds. Generative AI can help you to ensure your courses are inclusive and respectful of individual experiences and perspectives.

Here is an example of a prompt that creates a **lesson sequence:**

> <I teach Year 6 pupils (end of Key Stage 2) pupils in a London primary school. As part of the curriculum on Health and Wellbeing I would like to plan a series of six lessons on the topic of healthy eating. Pupils should know:
> - what constitutes a healthy diet (including understanding calories and other nutritional content)
> - the principles of planning and preparing a range of healthy meals
> - the characteristics of a poor diet and risks associated with unhealthy eating (including, for example, obesity and tooth decay) and other behaviours (for example the impact of alcohol on diet or health)
>
> Provide a set of 40-minute lesson plans, stating the objectives for each and adopting an interactive approach. Indicate where I might find additional resources that are suited to this age and stage. Note that I have no access to facilities for cooking or food preparation.>

Here is an example of a prompt that creates an **assignment** for students:

> <The Irish SPHE Senior Cycle curriculum in Social, Personal and Health Education (SPHE) has a topic on Negotiating and Managing Conflict. Create an assignment on this topic that is suitable for 16-year-old students. It should occupy two 40-minute lesson slots. Create a conflict scenario with a social or personal dimension suitable for this age and stage to support the assignment. I would like students to work in pairs. Provide instructions for the students. Provide a marking rubric to help me assess student performance.>

Here is an example of a prompt that creates an **assessment:**

<In the Scottish Qualifications Authority (SQA) National Qualification in National 5 Health and Food Technology, students are expected to explain the effects of the following diet-related diseases or conditions on health: obesity, dental caries, coronary heart disease, bowel disease, anaemia, high blood pressure, osteoporosis. Create a suitable assessment that would assess how well students understand these effects. Provide a marking scheme and indicate where each assessment item relates to the curriculum. I want the assessment to fit in a 40-minute class period.>

Here is an example of a prompt that creates **classroom activities** to enhance learning:

<The Ontario curriculum in Health and Physical Education for Grade 8 students requires that they 'demonstrate the ability to apply health knowledge and social-emotional learning skills to make reasoned decisions and take appropriate actions relating to their personal health and well-being'. Suggest a set of interactive classroom activities suited to this age and stage that would enable students to evidence the ability described above. For each activity, list the steps students will take, any resources they might require and the relevance of the activity to the Ontario curriculum.>

Here is an example of a **help me understand** prompt that a teacher could use:

> <I have been assigned to teach a Year 9 (Key Stage 3) class in an academy school in England. My responsibility is for the relationships, sex and health education (RSHE) curriculum. I need help to develop my own understanding of this topic so that I can confidently teach it. Create an outline of the key topics with which I should be familiar when teaching a Year 9 class. Identify any resources such as training in mental health wellbeing that would be helpful to me, and what I would learn from accessing the recommended resources or training.>

Glossary

Artificial intelligence (AI): Computer systems and machines that are designed to perform tasks that would otherwise require human intelligence, such as visual perception, speech recognition, and decision-making.

Chatbot: An AI system designed to communicate with humans using natural language. Chatbots can answer student questions, tutor topics, or provide interactive learning.

ChatGPT: A conversational AI system developed by OpenAI that can understand natural language questions and provide human-like responses. Could be used for interactive tutoring.

Computer vision: The capability of AI systems to identify, analyse, and understand digital images and videos. Allows applications like facial recognition, object detection, and image generation.

Context window: The amount of textual information that an AI system can consider at any given time when processing language. The larger the context window, the more tokens an AI can analyse, leading to a more nuanced understanding.

Deep learning: A type of machine learning that uses neural networks, inspired by the human brain, to learn from large amounts of data. Widely used for advanced applications like computer vision and natural language processing.

Ethical AI: AI systems designed and used in accordance with ethical principles like transparency, fairness, accountability and respect for human values. Critical for the safe use of AI in education.

Expert systems: AI systems designed to reproduce and automate the
decision-making ability of a human expert in a specific domain. Could tutor students in specialised subjects.

Explainable AI: AI systems whose decisions and predictions can be understood and interpreted by humans. Important for building teacher and student trust in AI tools.

Generative AI (GenAI): AI models that can generate new content like text, images, video or audio that mimics the data they are trained on. Allows creative applications for education.

Hallucinations: AI hallucinations are incorrect or misleading results that AI models generate. These errors can be caused by a variety of factors, including insufficient training data, incorrect assumptions made by the model, or biases in the data used to train the model.

Large language models (LLMs): AI models like GPT-4 that are trained on very large amounts of text data, to enable them to understand and generate human-like language.

Machine learning: The capability of AI systems to learn from data that enables them to carry out tasks without being explicitly programmed. This technology underlies many current AI applications.

Natural language processing (NLP): The ability of AI systems to understand, interpret, and generate human languages. Enables applications like chatbots, text summarisation, and translation.

Prompt: An input given to an AI system, often in natural language, designed to provide context and elicit a desired response. For example, prompts for language models like ChatGPT provide a query or starting sentence to generate a relevant text response. Carefully crafted prompts allow users to tune model behaviour.

Prompt engineering: The practice of strategically constructing and optimising prompts to improve the performance and reliability of AI systems like large language models. Prompt engineering applies knowledge of model capabilities and limitations to guide output. Techniques include using start and stop sequences, examples, templates and instructions.

Text-to-image synthesis: The capability of AI systems to generate realistic images from text descriptions and prompts. Allows creation of custom visual aids.

Printed in Great Britain
by Amazon